THE PERFECT
DIABETIC DIET
AFTER 50

Cookbook with **100+ Quick & easy** Low carb,Low Sugar Recipes **With Pictures** for Seniors & Beginners with Prediabetes and Type 2 Diabetes.

Wait ! Before You Go....

Thank you for purchasing this book! As a token of my appreciation, I'm excited to offer you some exclusive free bonuses that will enhance your journey towards healthier Life after 50. These bonuses include:

Bonus #1
30 DAY MEAL PLAN

We had Created a 30 Day Meal Plan For Diabetics Over 50 with balanced nutrition and easy recipes so that you can maintain stable blood sugar and enjoy stress-free meals.

Doctor-approved and tailored for your age, so that you can feel vibrant and in control of your diabetes.

Bonus #2
GROCERY LIST

Introducing our comprehensive Grocery Shopping List designed for effortless shopping, with Amazon links so that you can easily find and purchase all recommended ingredients.

Save time and enjoy one-click shopping so that you can focus on preparing healthy, delicious meals without the hassle.

Bonus #3
WORKSHEET

Introducing our Blood Sugar Tracking Worksheet, designed for easy and accurate logging so that you can monitor your blood sugar levels effortlessly.

Track consistently so that you can make informed decisions and maintain better control over your diabetes.

This is a Printable File , You can Get it Print From the Market.

Scan the QR Code Below !

To Download Your **Exclusive Bonuses**

YOUR OPINION MATTERS!

Hey Readers,

If you enjoyed reading this book, please take a moment to leave a review on Amazon. Writing this book took a lot of time and effort, and your review would be incredibly motivating for me to create more content that helps solve your problems.

Your feedback also helps me improve my products and better serve you in the future.

To leave your feedback:

1. Open your camera app
2. Point your mobile device at the QR code below
3. The review page will appear in your web browser

Thank you for your support!

TABLE OF CONTENTS

TABLE OF CONTENTS

TABLE OF CONTENTS

TABLE OF CONTENTS

TABLE OF CONTENTS

TABLE OF CONTENTS

INTRODUCTION

Welcome to the "Diabetic Diet After 50 Cookbook"! As we dive into this cooking adventure together, let's start by talking about diabetes. It's not just a health issue; it's something many people deal with every day.

Diabetes messes with how your body handles sugar, and if you don't keep it in check, it can lead to some serious health problems.

Now, let's unravel the mystery of how diabetes impacts your daily life and the strategies to navigate its complexities

1) OVERVIEW OF DIABETES

Diabetes is like a puzzle; it's a condition where your blood sugar levels are out of whack.

Sometimes your body doesn't make enough insulin (a hormone that helps control blood sugar), or it doesn't use it the right way. It's a tricky balance.

Ever wondered how these different types of diabetes impact your body in unique ways?

2) DEFINITION AND TYPES (TYPE 1, TYPE 2, GESTATIONAL)

Think of diabetes like a family with different members. Type 1 diabetes is like the kid who needs insulin shots because their body doesn't make enough.

Type 2 diabetes usually shows up later in life, and it's often because of things like eating too much junk food or not moving around enough.

Gestational diabetes happens during pregnancy and can affect both mom and baby. Now Let's see How Diet Plays an Important role in Managing Diabetes

3) IMPORTANCE OF DIET IN DIABETES MANAGEMENT

When it comes to dealing with diabetes, what you eat matters a lot. It's like fuel for your body, and the wrong kind can mess things up. Eating healthy stuff like fruits, veggies, and whole grains can help keep your blood sugar levels steady.

Watching how much you eat and staying active are also super important.

Ever wondered why making dietary changes becomes crucial after the age of 50, especially in the context of managing diabetes effectively? Let see

2) DEFINITION AND TYPES (TYPE 1, TYPE 2, GESTATIONAL)

Think of diabetes like a family with different members. Type 1 diabetes is like the kid who needs insulin shots because their body doesn't make enough.

Type 2 diabetes usually shows up later in life, and it's often because of things like eating too much junk food or not moving around enough.

Gestational diabetes happens during pregnancy and can affect both mom and baby. Now Let's see How Diet Plays an Important role in Managing Diabetes

IMPORTANCE OF DIETARY CHANGES AFTER 50

1) AGING AND METABOLISM

As we get older, our bodies change in many ways, including how we process food. It's like our metabolism – the way we burn calories – starts to slow down.

This means that if we keep eating the same way we did when we were younger, we might end up putting on extra weight or having trouble controlling our blood sugar levels. So, it's essential to pay attention to what we eat as we age.

2) INCREASED RISK FACTORS

Getting older also comes with a higher risk of certain health issues, like heart disease, high blood pressure, and yes, diabetes.

That's why it's extra important to take care of ourselves, especially when it comes to our diet. Eating the right foods can help lower our risk of developing these problems and keep us feeling our best as we age.

Curious why a diabetic diet holds significant benefits, especially for older adults, in mitigating health risks associated with aging?

3) BENEFITS OF A DIABETIC DIET FOR OLDER ADULTS

Now, you might be wondering, "What's so special about a diabetic diet?" Well, for starters, it's not just for people with diabetes.

A diabetic diet is all about eating foods that are good for you – things like fruits, veggies, whole grains, lean proteins, and healthy fats.

These foods can help keep your blood sugar levels steady, give you more energy, and even help you manage your weight. Plus, they taste pretty darn good too!

So, if you're over 50 and looking to stay healthy and feel great, paying attention to your diet is key.

Making simple changes like eating more veggies, watching your portion sizes, and staying active can go a long way toward keeping you happy and healthy for years to come.

It is also Important To Understand Diabetes In detail what are it's Risk Factors ?,What are its Symptoms & How It Can be Diagnosed Properly. Lets Go to Chapter 1

CHAPTER 1

UNDERSTANDING DIABETES

WHAT IS DIABETES?

Diabetes is like a glitch in your body's sugar-handling system. Normally, when you eat, your body breaks down food into sugar (also called glucose), which is a source of energy.

But when you have diabetes, something goes wrong with this process, and your blood sugar levels can get too high. It's like your body's sugar thermostat isn't working correctly.

CAUSES AND RISK FACTORS

A) GENETIC FACTORS

Ever heard the saying, "It runs in the family"? Well, that can be true for diabetes too. If you have family members with diabetes, you might be more likely to get it too.

It's like there's a genetic blueprint that can make you more prone to developing diabetes.

B) LIFESTYLE FACTORS

But genetics isn't the only player in this game. Lifestyle choices also play a big role. Things like eating too much junk food, not getting enough exercise, and carrying around extra weight can increase your chances of developing diabetes.

It's like your habits can either protect you from diabetes or make you more vulnerable to it.

SYMPTOMS AND DIAGNOSIS

A) COMMON SYMPTOMS

So, how do you know if you've got diabetes? There are some telltale signs to watch out for, like feeling thirsty all the time, needing to pee a lot – especially at night, feeling tired all the time, and having blurry vision.

It's like your body's way of waving a red flag to get your attention.

B) DIAGNOSTIC TESTS

But don't panic if you have some of these symptoms; they could be caused by other things too. To know for sure if you have diabetes, you'll need to see a doctor who can run some tests.

These might include a blood sugar test, where they check how much sugar is floating around in your blood, or an A1C test, which gives a snapshot of your blood sugar levels over the past few months.

It's like putting together puzzle pieces to get the full picture of what's going on in your body.Understanding diabetes is the first step toward managing it effectively.

By knowing the causes, risk factors, symptoms, and how it's diagnosed, you can take control of your health and make informed decisions about your care.

So, if you suspect you might have diabetes or want to learn more about it, don't hesitate to reach out to your healthcare provider.

They're there to help you navigate this journey and support you every step of the way.

In Chapter 2, You will Get to Know ,What strategies can individuals with diabetes use to incorporate foods with a lower glycemic index into their diets?

CHAPTER 2

BASICS OF A DIABETIC DIET

PRINCIPLES OF A DIABETIC DIET

A) BALANCED MEALS

Think of your plate like a colorful palette – you want a bit of everything to make it just right. A balanced meal for someone with diabetes includes a mix of carbohydrates, proteins, and healthy fats.

Carbs give you energy, protein helps you feel full and repairs your body, and fats keep your skin and hair healthy. It's like a symphony where every instrument plays its part to create harmony.

B) PORTION CONTROL

Imagine your stomach is like a treasure chest – you don't want to overload it with too much booty. Portion control is about keeping an eye on how much you eat to make sure you're not overdoing it.

It's like serving yourself just enough to satisfy your hunger without overstuffing yourself like a Thanksgiving turkey.

GLYCEMIC INDEX AND GLYCEMIC LOAD

Now, let's talk about sugar. Not all carbs are created equal – some make your blood sugar levels shoot up like a rocket, while others keep them steady like a calm sea.

The glycemic index (GI) and glycemic load (GL) are like maps that help you navigate the carb jungle. Foods with a low GI or GL release sugar into your bloodstream slowly, while high GI or GL foods cause a quick spike.

It's like choosing the scenic route instead of the expressway to keep your blood sugar levels on an even keel.

CARBOHYDRATE COUNTING

Carbs can be sneaky little critters hiding in your food, so it's essential to keep tabs on them.

Carbohydrate counting is like playing detective – you read food labels, measure servings, and track your intake to know exactly how many carbs you're eating.

It's like having a roadmap to help you stay on course and avoid unexpected blood sugar surprises.

CARBOHYDRATE COUNTING

Carbs can be sneaky little critters hiding in your food, so it's essential to keep tabs on them.

Carbohydrate counting is like playing detective – you read food labels, measure servings, and track your intake to know exactly how many carbs you're eating.

It's like having a roadmap to help you stay on course and avoid unexpected blood sugar surprises.

READING NUTRITION LABELS

Nutrition labels are like cheat sheets that tell you everything you need to know about a food's nutritional value. Paying attention to things like total carbs, fiber, and serving size can help you make smart choices and keep your blood sugar levels in check.

It's like having a secret decoder ring that helps you decipher which foods are your allies and which are your foes.

Mastering the basics of a diabetic diet is like learning the ABCs – it sets the foundation for your journey toward better health and blood sugar control.

By embracing principles like balanced meals, portion control, understanding the glycemic index, carbohydrate counting, and reading nutrition labels, you'll be equipped with the tools you need to make informed dietary choices and thrive with diabetes.

Ever wondered why some foods leave you feeling energized while others drag you down?
In chapter 3 You will Discover the Foods to Include In Your Diet & Chapter 4 which Foods to avoid During Diabetes.

CHAPTER 3
FOODS TO INCLUDE

1) NON-STARCHY VEGETABLES

Think of non-starchy veggies as the superheroes of your plate – they're packed with vitamins, minerals, and fiber but low in carbs and calories.

Load up on leafy greens like spinach and kale, crunchy veggies like broccoli and peppers, and colorful gems like carrots and tomatoes. It's like giving your body a nutrient-rich power-up to keep it running like a well-oiled machine.

2) WHOLE GRAINS

Whole grains are like the sturdy foundation of a house – they provide a steady source of energy and keep you feeling full and satisfied.

Swap refined grains like white bread and pasta for whole grain options like brown rice, quinoa, and whole wheat bread. It's like upgrading from a flimsy tent to a solid fortress to keep your blood sugar levels stable and your belly happy.

3) LEAN PROTEINS

Proteins are like the building blocks of your body – they help repair tissues, build muscle, and keep you feeling full for longer.

Choose lean proteins like skinless poultry, fish, tofu, beans, and lentils. It's like giving your body the tools it needs to stay strong and resilient, without weighing it down with excess fat and calories.

4) HEALTHY FATS

Fat is like the unsung hero of your diet – it's essential for absorbing vitamins, supporting cell growth, and providing long-lasting energy.

Opt for healthy fats like olive oil, avocado, nuts, and seeds, which can help improve cholesterol levels and protect your heart. It's like giving your body a hug from the inside out, nourishing it with the good stuff it craves.

5) FRUITS WITH LOW GLYCEMIC INDEX

Fruits are like nature's candy – sweet, juicy, and bursting with flavor. But not all fruits are created equal when it comes to managing blood sugar levels.

Choose fruits with a low glycemic index, like berries, apples, oranges, and pears, which release sugar into your bloodstream slowly. It's like enjoying a sweet treat without sending your blood sugar on a rollercoaster ride.

6) DAIRY AND ALTERNATIVES

Dairy products are like the Swiss Army knife of nutrition – they're versatile, providing essential nutrients like calcium, vitamin D, and protein.

Opt for low-fat or fat-free options like milk, yogurt, and cheese, or try dairy alternatives like almond milk or soy yogurt if you're lactose intolerant or vegan.

It's like keeping your bones strong and your taste buds happy, no matter your dietary preferences.

By including a variety of these nutrient-rich foods in your diet, you'll nourish your body from the inside out, support stable blood sugar levels, and enjoy a delicious and satisfying eating experience.

So, let's fill our plates with the good stuff and savor every bite of our journey to better health!

CHAPTER 4
FOODS TO AVOID OR LIMIT

1) SUGARY FOODS AND BEVERAGES

Imagine sugary treats and drinks as the sweet talkers at a party – they might seem charming, but they can lead you down a sugary path.

It's like being tempted by the dessert table at every turn. To stay grounded, consider limiting or passing on goodies like candies, sodas, fruit juices loaded with sugar, sugary snacks, and those irresistible pastries.

Instead, opt for naturally sweet options like fresh fruits or quench your thirst with water infused with a splash of flavor. It's like sidestepping a sugary dance and choosing a refreshing breeze instead.

2) REFINED CARBOHYDRATES

Refined carbs are like quick fixes – they give you a burst of energy, but it fizzles out just as fast, leaving you craving more.

These sneaky troublemakers, found in white bread, sugary cereals, and processed snacks, can send your blood sugar levels on a rollercoaster ride.

So, swap them out for whole grain alternatives like brown rice, oats, and whole grain pasta that offer a steady stream of energy without the crash.

It's like trading in a fleeting sugar rush for a sustained energy boost that keeps you going strong.

3) TRANS FATS AND SATURATED FATS

Trans fats and saturated fats are like the indulgent treats you can't resist – they're delicious but not so good for you in large doses.

Skip the deep-fried temptations, buttery spreads, and fatty cuts of meat that can harm your heart health.

Instead, choose heart-healthy fats like olive oil, avocados, and nuts that nourish your body and keep your ticker ticking. It's like indulging in a little treat now and then but making sure it's worth it in the long run.

4) HIGH-SODIUM FOODS

Sodium is like the silent troublemaker – it can sneak into your diet and wreak havoc on your health without you even realizing it.

Watch out for salty snacks, canned soups, processed meats, and fast food items that are loaded with sodium and can raise your blood pressure.

Instead, add flavor to your meals with herbs, spices, and citrus to satisfy your taste buds without the extra salt. It's like discovering a world of flavor that doesn't come with a hidden health cost.

5) ALCOHOL

Alcohol is like the life of the party – it can be fun in moderation, but overindulging can lead to trouble.

Keep your alcohol intake in check and enjoy it alongside a meal to help moderate its effects on your blood sugar levels. It's like finding the right balance between enjoying a drink and knowing when to say when.

By making mindful choices and avoiding or limiting these less-than-ideal foods and beverages, you'll set yourself up for success in managing your diabetes and supporting your overall health.

So, let's wave goodbye to these dietary distractions and welcome in a world of delicious, diabetes-friendly options that nourish both body and soul!

BREAKFAST
RECIPES

PREP TIME

10 Minutes

COOKING TIME

20 Minutes

SERVINGS

1

1) Greek Yogurt
with Berries and Nuts

Creamy Greek Yogurt Paired With Vibrant Berries And Crunchy Nuts Makes For A Satisfying And Nutritious Breakfast That's Quick To Whip Up.

INGREDIENTS

- 1/2 cup Greek yogurt
- 1/4 cup mixed berries (such as strawberries, blueberries, and raspberries)
- 2 tablespoons chopped nuts (such as almonds or walnuts)

PROCEDURE

1. Spoon the Greek yogurt into a bowl or glass.
2. Top with mixed berries.
3. Sprinkle chopped nuts over the berries.
4. Enjoy your delicious and nutritious breakfast!

NUTRITIONAL INFORMATION (PER SERVING)

Calories: 200 | Carbohydrates: 15g | Protein: 18g | Fat: 9g | Fiber: 4g

PREP TIME

10 Minutes

COOKING TIME

5 Minutes

SERVINGS

1

2) Scrambled Eggs
with Spinach and Feta

Fluffy scrambled eggs combined with nutritious spinach and flavorful feta cheese create a savory breakfast option that's both tasty and simple to prepare.

INGREDIENTS

- 2 eggs
- 1 cup fresh spinach leaves
- 1/4 cup crumbled feta cheese
- Salt and pepper to taste

PROCEDURE

1. In a bowl, beat the eggs with salt and pepper.
2. Heat a non-stick skillet over medium heat and add the beaten eggs.
3. As the eggs begin to set, add the spinach leaves and feta cheese.
4. Continue to cook, stirring gently, until the eggs are cooked through and the spinach is wilted.
5. Serve hot and enjoy your nutritious breakfast!

NUTRITIONAL INFORMATION (PER SERVING)

Calories: 290 | Carbohydrates: 4g | Protein: 21g | Fat: 20g | Fiber: 2g

PREP TIME

5 Minutes

COOKING TIME

0 Minutes

SERVINGS

1

3) Avocado Toast
on Whole Grain Bread

Creamy avocado spread over hearty whole grain bread makes for a delicious and filling breakfast option that's packed with healthy fats and fiber.

INGREDIENTS

- 1 slice whole grain bread, toasted
- 1/2 ripe avocado
- Pinch of salt
- Pinch of red pepper flakes (optional)

PROCEDURE

1. Mash the ripe avocado in a bowl with a fork until smooth.
2. Season with a pinch of salt and red pepper flakes, if desired.
3. Spread the mashed avocado evenly onto the toasted whole grain bread.
4. Serve immediately and enjoy your nutritious and delicious avocado toast!

NUTRITIONAL INFORMATION (PER SERVING)

Calories: 220 | Carbohydrates: 17g | Protein: 4g | Fat: 15g | Fiber: 7g

PREP TIME

5 Minutes

COOKING TIME

0 Minutes

SERVINGS

1

4) Chia Seed Pudding
with Almond Milk and Fresh Fruit

Chia seed pudding made with creamy almond milk and topped with fresh fruit is a sweet and satisfying breakfast option that's loaded with fiber and antioxidants.

INGREDIENTS

- 2 tablespoons chia seeds
- 1/2 cup unsweetened almond milk
- 1/4 teaspoon vanilla extract
- Fresh fruit for topping (such as sliced strawberries, blueberries, or raspberries)

PROCEDURE

1. In a bowl, combine the chia seeds, almond milk, and vanilla extract.
2. Stir well to combine, then cover and refrigerate for at least 2 hours or overnight, until thickened.
3. Once the chia pudding has thickened, stir again to break up any clumps.
4. Transfer the pudding to a serving dish and top with fresh fruit.
5. Serve chilled and enjoy your nutritious and delicious chia seed pudding!

NUTRITIONAL INFORMATION (PER SERVING)

Calories: 180 | Carbohydrates: 16g | Protein: 5g | Fat: 11g | Fiber: 10g

PREP TIME

5 Minutes

COOKING TIME

5 Minutes

SERVINGS

1

5) Oatmeal
with Cinnamon and Walnuts

Warm oatmeal flavored with cinnamon and topped with crunchy walnuts is a comforting and nutritious breakfast choice that will keep you satisfied all morning long.

INGREDIENTS

- 1/2 cup old-fashioned oats
- 1 cup water or milk of your choice
- 1/2 teaspoon ground cinnamon
- 1 tablespoon chopped walnuts
- Optional: sweetener of your choice (such as honey or maple syrup)

PROCEDURE

1. In a small saucepan, bring the water or milk to a boil.
2. Stir in the oats and reduce the heat to low.
3. Cook, stirring occasionally, for about 5 minutes, or until the oatmeal reaches your desired consistency.
4. Stir in the ground cinnamon.
5. Transfer the oatmeal to a bowl and sprinkle with chopped walnuts.
6. Sweeten to taste, if desired.
7. Serve hot and enjoy your comforting and nutritious oatmeal!

NUTRITIONAL INFORMATION (PER SERVING)

Calories: 280 | Carbohydrates: 40g | Protein: 9g | Fat: 10g | Fiber: 7g

PREP TIME

5 Minutes

COOKING TIME

0Minutes

SERVINGS

1

6) Cottage Cheese
with Sliced Peaches

Creamy cottage cheese paired with sweet sliced peaches creates a light and refreshing breakfast option that's high in protein and perfect for busy mornings.

INGREDIENTS

- 1/2 cup cottage cheese
- 1 ripe peach, sliced
- Optional: drizzle of honey or sprinkle of cinnamon

PROCEDURE

1. Spoon the cottage cheese into a bowl.
2. Top with sliced peaches.
3. Drizzle with honey or sprinkle with cinnamon, if desired.
4. Serve chilled or at room temperature.
5. Enjoy your light and refreshing breakfast!

NUTRITIONAL INFORMATION (PER SERVING)

Calories: 180 | Carbohydrates: 21g | Protein: 15g | Fat: 3g | Fiber: 2g

7) Veggie Omelette

with Bell Peppers and Mushrooms

Fluffy eggs loaded with colourful bell peppers and earthy mushrooms make for a satisfying and nutritious breakfast that's bursting with flavour and packed with veggies.

INGREDIENTS

- 2 eggs
- 1/4 cup sliced bell peppers (any color)
- 1/4 cup sliced mushrooms
- Salt and pepper to taste
- Cooking spray or olive oil

PROCEDURE

1. In a bowl, beat the eggs with salt and pepper.
2. Heat a non-stick skillet over medium heat and lightly coat with cooking spray or olive oil.
3. Add the sliced bell peppers and mushrooms to the skillet and cook until softened, about 2-3 minutes.
4. Pour the beaten eggs over the veggies in the skillet.
5. Cook, lifting the edges of the omelette with a spatula and tilting the skillet to let the uncooked egg flow underneath, until the eggs are set.
6. Carefully fold the omelette in half and transfer to a plate.
7. Serve hot and enjoy your veggie-packed omelette!

NUTRITIONAL INFORMATION (PER SERVING)

Calories: 210 | Carbohydrates: 6g | Protein: 17g | Fat: 13g | Fiber: 2g

8) Smoothie
with Kale, Berries, and Greek Yogurt

A vibrant smoothie packed with nutrient-rich kale, antioxidant-packed berries, and creamy Greek yogurt is a refreshing and energizing way to start your day on a healthy note.

INGREDIENTS

- 1 cup fresh kale leaves, stems removed
- 1/2 cup mixed berries (such as strawberries, blueberries, and raspberries)
- 1/2 cup Greek yogurt
- 1/2 cup water or unsweetened almond milk
- Optional: honey or maple syrup to sweeten

PROCEDURE

1. In a blender, combine the kale, mixed berries, Greek yogurt, and water or almond milk.
2. Blend until smooth and creamy.
3. Sweeten to taste with honey or maple syrup, if desired.
4. Pour into a glass and enjoy your refreshing and nutrient-packed smoothie!

NUTRITIONAL INFORMATION (PER SERVING)

Calories: 210 | Carbohydrates: 6g | Protein: 17g | Fat: 13g | Fiber: 2g

PREP TIME

5 Minutes

COOKING TIME

0 Minutes

SERVINGS

1

9) Whole Grain Muffin

with Peanut Butter

A hearty whole grain English muffin topped with creamy peanut butter is a simple and satisfying breakfast option that provides a good balance of protein, healthy fats, and carbohydrates to fuel your morning.

INGREDIENTS

- 1 whole grain English muffin, split and toasted
- 2 tablespoons natural peanut butter

PROCEDURE

1. Spread the peanut butter evenly onto the toasted English muffin halves.
2. Serve immediately and enjoy your simple and satisfying breakfast!

NUTRITIONAL INFORMATION (PER SERVING)

Calories: 280 | Carbohydrates: 25g | Protein: 10g | Fat: 16g | Fiber: 5g

10) Quinoa Breakfast Bowl

with Almonds and Blueberries

A nutritious and filling breakfast bowl featuring protein-packed quinoa, crunchy almonds, and sweet blueberries is a delicious way to kickstart your day with a boost of energy and antioxidants.

INGREDIENTS

- 1/2 cup cooked quinoa
- 1/4 cup sliced almonds
- 1/4 cup fresh blueberries
- 1 tablespoon honey
- Optional: splash of milk or yogurt

PROCEDURE

1. In a bowl, combine the cooked quinoa, sliced almonds, and fresh blueberries.
2. Drizzle with honey and stir to combine.
3. If desired, add a splash of milk or yogurt for extra creaminess.
4. Serve warm or chilled and enjoy your nutritious and delicious quinoa breakfast bowl!

NUTRITIONAL INFORMATION (PER SERVING)

Calories: 280 | Carbohydrates: 25g | Protein: 10g | Fat: 16g | Fiber: 5g

PREP TIME

10 Minutes

COOKING TIME

20 Minutes

SERVINGS

6

11) Egg Muffins

with Turkey Sausage and Spinach

A delicious, protein-packed breakfast perfect for meal prepping. These egg muffins are easy to make and great for busy mornings.

INGREDIENTS

- 6 large eggs
- 1/2 cup cooked turkey sausage, crumbled
- 1 cup fresh spinach, chopped
- 1/4 cup milk (low-fat)
- 1/4 cup shredded cheddar cheese
- Salt and pepper to taste
- Cooking spray

PROCEDURE

1. Preheat your oven to 375°F (190°C). Spray a muffin tin with cooking spray.
2. In a large bowl, whisk the eggs and milk together. Season with salt and pepper.
3. Stir in the turkey sausage, spinach, and cheddar cheese.
4. Pour the mixture evenly into the muffin tin cups.
5. Bake for 20 minutes, or until the eggs are set and the tops are golden brown.
6. Allow to cool slightly before removing from the muffin tin.

NUTRITIONAL INFORMATION (PER SERVING)

100 calories, 7g protein, 1g carbs, 7g fat

12) Low-Carb Burrito
with Eggs and Avocado

A satisfying and nutritious breakfast burrito that's low in carbs and high in healthy fats and protein.

INGREDIENTS

- 2 large eggs
- 1 small avocado, sliced
- 1/4 cup shredded cheese
- 1/4 cup diced tomatoes
- 1 whole wheat tortilla (low-carb)
- Salt and pepper to taste
- Cooking spray

PROCEDURE

1. Heat a non-stick skillet over medium heat and spray with cooking spray.
2. Whisk the eggs in a bowl and season with salt and pepper. Pour into the skillet.
3. Cook the eggs, stirring occasionally, until scrambled and fully cooked.
4. Lay the tortilla flat and place the scrambled eggs in the center.
5. Top with avocado slices, shredded cheese, and diced tomatoes.
6. Roll up the tortilla, folding in the sides as you go. Serve warm.

NUTRITIONAL INFORMATION (PER SERVING)

320 calories, 18g protein, 10g carbs, 25g fat

13) Overnight Oats
with Chia Seeds and Fresh Berries

A quick and healthy breakfast that you can prepare the night before, perfect for a busy morning.

INGREDIENTS

- 1/2 cup rolled oats
- 1 cup almond milk (unsweetened)
- 1 tbsp chia seeds
- 1/2 cup fresh berries (strawberries, blueberries, or raspberries)
- 1 tsp honey or a sweetener of your choice (optional)

PROCEDURE

1. In a jar or bowl, combine the rolled oats, almond milk, and chia seeds.
2. Stir well to mix, then cover and refrigerate overnight.
3. In the morning, stir the oats again and top with fresh berries.
4. Add a drizzle of honey if desired.

NUTRITIONAL INFORMATION (PER SERVING)

250 calories, 8g protein, 40g carbs, 7g fat

14) Smoked Salmon

and Cream Cheese on Whole Grain Bagel

A classic combination that's both delicious and nutritious, ideal for a quick and healthy breakfast.

INGREDIENTS

- 1 whole grain bagel, halved and toasted
- 2 tbsp cream cheese (low-fat)
- 2 oz smoked salmon
- 1 tbsp capers
- 1 tbsp red onion, thinly sliced
- Fresh dill for garnish

PROCEDURE

1. Spread the cream cheese evenly over both halves of the toasted bagel.
2. Layer the smoked salmon on top of the cream cheese.
3. Sprinkle with capers and red onion slices.
4. Garnish with fresh dill and serve immediately.

NUTRITIONAL INFORMATION (PER SERVING)

350 calories, 20g protein, 40g carbs, 13g fat

15) Apple Slices

with Almond Butter

A simple yet satisfying snack or light breakfast, perfect for when you're on the go.

INGREDIENTS

- 1 medium apple, cored and sliced
- 2 tbsp almond butter

PROCEDURE

1. Arrange the apple slices on a plate.
2. Serve with almond butter for dipping or spread the almond butter on the apple slices.

NUTRITIONAL INFORMATION (PER SERVING)

200 calories, 4g protein, 26g carbs, 10g fat

16) Berry and Spinach
Smoothie Bowl

A vibrant and nutrient-packed smoothie bowl that's both delicious and energizing.

INGREDIENTS

- 1 cup spinach
- 1/2 cup frozen berries (strawberries, blueberries, or mixed)
- 1/2 banana
- 1/2 cup Greek yogurt (low-fat)
- 1/2 cup almond milk (unsweetened)
- 1 tbsp chia seeds
- 1 tbsp sliced almonds

PROCEDURE

1. In a blender, combine the spinach, frozen berries, banana, Greek yogurt, and almond milk. Blend until smooth.
2. Pour the smoothie into a bowl.
3. Top with chia seeds and sliced almonds. Serve immediately.

NUTRITIONAL INFORMATION (PER SERVING)

250 calories, 12g protein, 35g carbs, 8g fat

17) Zucchini Bread Muffins

(Low-Sugar)

Moist and flavorful muffins that are low in sugar and high in fiber, making them a healthy breakfast option.

INGREDIENTS

- 1 1/2 cups grated zucchini
- 1 1/2 cups whole wheat flour
- 1/2 cup almond flour
- 1/4 cup coconut sugar
- 1 tsp baking soda
- 1/2 tsp baking powder
- 1/2 tsp cinnamon
- 1/4 tsp salt
- 2 large eggs
- 1/2 cup unsweetened applesauce
- 1/4 cup olive oil
- 1 tsp vanilla extract

PROCEDURE

1. Preheat your oven to 350°F (175°C). Line a muffin tin with paper liners or spray with cooking spray.
2. In a large bowl, combine the whole wheat flour, almond flour, coconut sugar, baking soda, baking powder, cinnamon, and salt.
3. In another bowl, whisk together the eggs, applesauce, olive oil, and vanilla extract.
4. Add the wet ingredients to the dry ingredients and stir until just combined. Fold in the grated zucchini.
5. Divide the batter evenly among the muffin cups.
6. Bake for 20-25 minutes, or until a toothpick inserted into the center comes out clean.
7. Allow to cool in the tin for 5 minutes, then transfer to a wire rack to cool completely.

NUTRITIONAL INFORMATION (PER SERVING)

120 calories, 3g protein, 15g carbs, 6g fat

18) Poached Eggs
on Whole Wheat Toast

A classic and simple breakfast that's quick to make and packed with protein.

INGREDIENTS

- 2 large eggs
- 1 slice whole wheat bread, toasted
- Salt and pepper to taste
- Fresh herbs for garnish (optional)

PROCEDURE

1. Fill a medium saucepan with about 3 inches of water and bring to a gentle simmer.
2. Crack each egg into a small bowl, then gently slide the eggs into the simmering water.
3. Poach the eggs for 3-4 minutes, or until the whites are set but the yolks are still runny.
4. Use a slotted spoon to remove the eggs from the water and place them on a paper towel to drain briefly.
5. Place the poached eggs on the toasted whole wheat bread.
6. Season with salt and pepper and garnish with fresh herbs if desired. Serve immediately.

NUTRITIONAL INFORMATION (PER SERVING)

120 calories, 3g protein, 15g carbs, 6g fat

19) Tomato and Avocado Salad

with Hard-Boiled Eggs

A refreshing and nutritious salad that's perfect for breakfast or a light lunch.

INGREDIENTS

- 2 large eggs
- 1 ripe avocado, diced
- 1 cup cherry tomatoes, halved
- 1/4 red onion, thinly sliced
- 1 tbsp olive oil
- 1 tbsp lemon juice
- Salt and pepper to taste
- Fresh basil leaves for garnish

PROCEDURE

1. Place the eggs in a saucepan and cover with water. Bring to a boil, then reduce heat and simmer for 9-10 minutes. Transfer to a bowl of ice water to cool, then peel and quarter the eggs.
2. In a large bowl, combine the diced avocado, cherry tomatoes, and red onion.
3. Drizzle with olive oil and lemon juice, then season with salt and pepper. Toss gently to combine.
4. Divide the salad between two plates and top each with the quartered eggs.
5. Garnish with fresh basil leaves and serve immediately.

NUTRITIONAL INFORMATION (PER SERVING)

250 calories, 10g protein, 12g carbs, 20g fat

PREP TIME

5 Minutes

COOKING TIME

0 Minutes

SERVINGS

1

20) Cinnamon-Spiced Cottage Cheese
with Pear Slices

A protein-packed breakfast that's quick, easy, and full of flavor.

INGREDIENTS

- 1 cup cottage cheese (low-fat)
- 1 medium pear, cored and sliced
- 1/2 tsp ground cinnamon
- 1 tsp honey (optional)

PROCEDURE

1. Spoon the cottage cheese into a bowl.
2. Arrange the pear slices on top of the cottage cheese.
3. Sprinkle with ground cinnamon and drizzle with honey if desired.
4. Serve immediately.

NUTRITIONAL INFORMATION (PER SERVING)

200 calories, 15g protein, 28g carbs, 3g fat

21) Cauliflower Hash Browns
with Turkey Bacon

A delicious and healthy alternative to traditional hash browns, these cauliflower hash browns are paired perfectly with turkey bacon for a satisfying breakfast.

INGREDIENTS

- 1 small head of cauliflower, grated
- 1 egg
- 1/4 cup almond flour
- 1/4 cup grated Parmesan cheese
- 1/4 teaspoon garlic powder
- 1/4 teaspoon onion powder
- Salt and pepper to taste
- 4 slices turkey bacon

PROCEDURE

1. Preheat the oven to 400°F (200°C).
2. Place the grated cauliflower in a clean kitchen towel and squeeze out excess moisture.
3. In a bowl, mix cauliflower, egg, almond flour, Parmesan cheese, garlic powder, onion powder, salt, and pepper.
4. Form the mixture into small patties and place them on a baking sheet lined with parchment paper.
5. Bake for 15-20 minutes until golden brown and crispy.
6. While the hash browns are baking, cook the turkey bacon in a skillet over medium heat until crispy.
7. Serve the hash browns with turkey bacon on the side.

NUTRITIONAL INFORMATION (PER SERVING)

150 calories, 10g protein, 8g fat, 8g carbohydrates

22) Pumpkin Smoothie
with Greek Yogurt and Cinnamon

This creamy and delicious pumpkin smoothie is perfect for a quick and nutritious breakfast.

INGREDIENTS

- 1 cup canned pumpkin
- 1 cup Greek yogurt
- 1/2 cup unsweetened almond milk
- 1 tablespoon honey
- 1/2 teaspoon ground cinnamon
- 1/4 teaspoon ground nutmeg
- Ice cubes

PROCEDURE

1. Combine pumpkin, Greek yogurt, almond milk, honey, cinnamon, nutmeg, and a handful of ice cubes in a blender.
2. Blend until smooth and creamy.
3. Pour into glasses and serve immediately.

NUTRITIONAL INFORMATION (PER SERVING)

120 calories, 8g protein, 2g fat, 18g carbohydrates

23) Ricotta Cheese
with Mixed Berries

A light and refreshing breakfast option, this dish pairs creamy ricotta cheese with a medley of fresh berries.

INGREDIENTS

- 1 cup ricotta cheese
- 1 cup mixed fresh berries (strawberries, blueberries, raspberries)
- 1 tablespoon honey
- 1/2 teaspoon vanilla extract

PROCEDURE

1. In a bowl, mix ricotta cheese, honey, and vanilla extract until smooth.
2. Divide the ricotta mixture between two bowls.
3. Top each bowl with mixed berries.
4. Serve immediately.

NUTRITIONAL INFORMATION (PER SERVING)

120 calories, 8g protein, 2g fat, 18g carbohydrates

24) Almond Flour Pancakes

with Fresh Raspberries

These fluffy almond flour pancakes are low in carbs and high in flavor, topped with fresh raspberries for a sweet touch.

INGREDIENTS

- 1 cup almond flour
- 1 teaspoon baking powder
- 2 eggs
- 1/4 cup unsweetened almond milk
- 1 tablespoon honey
- 1/2 teaspoon vanilla extract
- 1/2 cup fresh raspberries

PROCEDURE

1. In a bowl, whisk together almond flour and baking powder.
2. In another bowl, beat the eggs and then mix in almond milk, honey, and vanilla extract.
3. Combine the wet and dry ingredients and mix until smooth.
4. Heat a non-stick skillet over medium heat and pour 1/4 cup of batter for each pancake.
5. Cook until bubbles form on the surface, then flip and cook until golden brown.
6. Serve pancakes topped with fresh raspberries.

NUTRITIONAL INFORMATION (PER SERVING)

220 calories, 10g protein, 15g fat, 10g carbohydrates

25) Turkey and Veggie

Breakfast Skille

A hearty and nutritious breakfast skillet loaded with turkey and fresh vegetables.

INGREDIENTS

- 1 tablespoon olive oil
- 1/2 pound ground turkey
- 1 bell pepper, diced
- 1 small zucchini, diced
- 1/2 cup cherry tomatoes, halved
- 1/2 teaspoon garlic powder
- Salt and pepper to taste
- 2 tablespoons chopped fresh parsley

PROCEDURE

1. Heat olive oil in a large skillet over medium heat.
2. Add ground turkey and cook until browned.
3. Add bell pepper, zucchini, and cherry tomatoes to the skillet.
4. Season with garlic powder, salt, and pepper.
5. Cook until vegetables are tender.
6. Sprinkle with fresh parsley before serving.

NUTRITIONAL INFORMATION (PER SERVING)

250 calories, 25g protein, 10g fat, 10g carbohydrates

PREP TIME

10 Minutes

COOKING TIME

20 Minutes

SERVINGS

2

26) Portobello Mushrooms

Spinach and Cheese Stuffed

A delicious and nutritious breakfast that is perfect for starting your day with a healthy dose of vegetables and protein.

INGREDIENTS

- 4 large Portobello mushrooms
- 1 cup fresh spinach, chopped
- 1/2 cup low-fat cottage cheese
- 1/4 cup grated Parmesan cheese
- 1 garlic clove, minced
- 1 tablespoon olive oil
- Salt and pepper to taste

PROCEDURE

1. Preheat your oven to 375°F (190°C).
2. Clean the Portobello mushrooms and remove the stems.
3. In a skillet, heat the olive oil over medium heat. Add garlic and sauté for 1 minute.
4. Add the chopped spinach and cook until wilted, about 2-3 minutes.
5. Remove from heat and mix in the cottage cheese and Parmesan cheese. Season with salt and pepper.
6. Stuff each mushroom with the spinach mixture.
7. Place the stuffed mushrooms on a baking sheet and bake for 15-20 minutes, or until the mushrooms are tender.

NUTRITIONAL INFORMATION (PER SERVING)

Calories: 180, Carbs: 12g, Protein: 14g, Fat: 10g

PREP TIME

10 Minutes

COOKING TIME

10 Minutes

SERVINGS

2

27) Banana Oatmeal Pancakes

These pancakes are a healthy twist on a classic breakfast favorite, perfect for a satisfying and energy-boosting morning meal.

INGREDIENTS

- 1 ripe banana
- 1 cup rolled oats
- 2 eggs
- 1/2 teaspoon baking powder
- 1/2 teaspoon vanilla extract
- 1/4 teaspoon ground cinnamon
- Cooking spray or a small amount of butter for the pan

PROCEDURE

1. In a blender, combine the banana, oats, eggs, baking powder, vanilla extract, and cinnamon. Blend until smooth.
2. Heat a non-stick skillet over medium heat and lightly coat with cooking spray or butter.
3. Pour 1/4 cup of batter onto the skillet for each pancake.
4. Cook for 2-3 minutes on each side, or until golden brown and cooked through.
5. Serve warm with your favorite toppings, such as fresh berries or a drizzle of maple syrup.

NUTRITIONAL INFORMATION (PER SERVING)

Calories: 220, Carbs: 30g, Protein: 10g, Fat: 6g

28) Cucumber and Smoked Salmon

Roll-Ups

A light and refreshing breakfast option that combines the crispness of cucumber with the rich flavor of smoked salmon.

INGREDIENTS

- 1 large cucumber
- 4 ounces smoked salmon
- 2 tablespoons low-fat cream cheese
- 1 tablespoon fresh dill, chopped
- 1 teaspoon lemon juice
- Salt and pepper to taste

PROCEDURE

1. Using a vegetable peeler, slice the cucumber lengthwise into thin strips.
2. In a small bowl, mix the cream cheese, dill, lemon juice, salt, and pepper.
3. Spread a thin layer of the cream cheese mixture onto each cucumber strip.
4. Place a small piece of smoked salmon on top of the cream cheese.
5. Roll up the cucumber strips and secure with a toothpick if necessary.
6. Serve immediately.

NUTRITIONAL INFORMATION (PER SERVING)

Calories: 150, Carbs: 5g, Protein: 12g, Fat: 10g

29) Black Bean and Avocado

Breakfast Bowl

A hearty and flavorful breakfast bowl packed with protein, healthy fats, and fiber to keep you full and energized.

INGREDIENTS

- 1 cup canned black beans, drained and rinsed
- 1 ripe avocado, diced
- 1/2 cup cherry tomatoes, halved
- 2 tablespoons red onion, finely chopped
- 1 tablespoon fresh cilantro, chopped
- 1 tablespoon lime juice
- Salt and pepper to taste

PROCEDURE

1. In a medium bowl, combine the black beans, avocado, cherry tomatoes, red onion, and cilantro.
2. Drizzle with lime juice and season with salt and pepper.
3. Toss gently to combine all ingredients.
4. Serve immediately, either alone or with a side of whole grain toast.

NUTRITIONAL INFORMATION (PER SERVING)

Calories: 250, Carbs: 30g, Protein: 8g, Fat: 15g

PREP TIME

10 Minutes

COOKING TIME

15 Minutes

SERVINGS

2

30) Whole Grain Waffles

with Greek Yogurt and Fresh Fruit

A wholesome and satisfying breakfast that pairs crispy whole grain waffles with creamy Greek yogurt and fresh fruit.

INGREDIENTS

- 1 cup whole grain waffle mix
- 1/2 cup water (or as directed by waffle mix package)
- 1/2 cup plain Greek yogurt
- 1/2 cup fresh berries (strawberries, blueberries, raspberries)
- 1 tablespoon honey (optional)

PROCEDURE

1. Preheat your waffle iron according to the manufacturer's instructions.
2. In a bowl, mix the waffle mix with water until smooth.
3. Pour the batter onto the preheated waffle iron and cook until golden brown and crispy.
4. Top each waffle with a dollop of Greek yogurt and a handful of fresh berries.
5. Drizzle with honey if desired and serve immediately.

NUTRITIONAL INFORMATION (PER SERVING)

Calories: 300, Carbs: 45g, Protein: 12g, Fat: 8g

LUNCH & DINNER
RECIPES

PREP TIME

15 Minutes

COOKING TIME

10 Minutes

SERVINGS

4

1) Grilled Chicken Salad

with Mixed Greens and Balsamic Vinaigrette

A refreshing and healthy salad packed with lean protein and fresh vegetables, perfect for a light lunch or dinner.

INGREDIENTS

- 2 boneless, skinless chicken breasts
- 8 cups mixed salad greens
- 1 cup cherry tomatoes, halved
- 1 cucumber, sliced
- 1/4 cup red onion, thinly sliced
- 1/4 cup crumbled feta cheese (optional)
- 2 tablespoons olive oil
- Salt and pepper to taste

For the Balsamic Vinaigrette:

- 1/4 cup balsamic vinegar
- 1/4 cup olive oil
- 1 teaspoon Dijon mustard
- 1 garlic clove, minced
- Salt and pepper to taste

PROCEDURE

1. Preheat the grill to medium-high heat.
2. Season the chicken breasts with olive oil, salt, and pepper.
3. Grill the chicken for about 5 minutes on each side or until fully cooked. Let it rest for 5 minutes, then slice thinly.
4. In a large bowl, combine mixed greens, cherry tomatoes, cucumber, and red onion.
5. In a small bowl, whisk together the balsamic vinegar, olive oil, Dijon mustard, garlic, salt, and pepper.
6. Drizzle the vinaigrette over the salad and toss to coat.
7. Top the salad with grilled chicken slices and crumbled feta cheese if using.
8. Serve immediately.

NUTRITIONAL INFORMATION (PER SERVING)

320 calories, 15g fat, 12g carbohydrates, 35g protein

2) Baked Salmon

with Asparagus and Quinoa

A nutritious and flavorful meal featuring heart-healthy salmon, roasted asparagus, and protein-packed quinoa.

INGREDIENTS

- 4 salmon fillets (about 6 oz each)
- 1 bunch asparagus, trimmed
- 1 cup quinoa
- 2 cups water or low-sodium chicken broth
- 2 tablespoons olive oil
- 1 lemon, sliced
- Salt and pepper to taste

PROCEDURE

1. Preheat the oven to 400°F (200°C).
2. Place the salmon fillets on a baking sheet lined with parchment paper. Arrange the asparagus around the salmon.
3. Drizzle olive oil over the salmon and asparagus. Season with salt and pepper.
4. Top the salmon with lemon slices.
5. Bake for 15-20 minutes, or until the salmon is cooked through and flakes easily with a fork.
6. Meanwhile, rinse the quinoa under cold water. In a medium saucepan, bring 2 cups of water or broth to a boil. Add the quinoa, reduce heat, cover, and simmer for 15 minutes or until the water is absorbed.
7. Fluff the quinoa with a fork and divide among plates. Serve with the baked salmon and asparagus.

NUTRITIONAL INFORMATION (PER SERVING)

450 calories, 18g fat, 29g carbohydrates, 42g protein

3) Turkey and Veggie Lettuce Wraps

These turkey and veggie lettuce wraps are a tasty, low-carb alternative to traditional wraps, perfect for a quick meal.

INGREDIENTS

- 1 lb ground turkey
- 1 tablespoon olive oil
- 1 red bell pepper, diced
- 1 zucchini, diced
- 1 carrot, grated
- 2 garlic cloves, minced
- 1/4 cup low-sodium soy sauce
- 1 tablespoon rice vinegar
- 1 teaspoon sesame oil
- 8 large lettuce leaves (such as romaine or butter lettuce)

PROCEDURE

1. In a large skillet, heat olive oil over medium-high heat. Add ground turkey and cook until browned, breaking it up with a spoon.
2. Add red bell pepper, zucchini, carrot, and garlic to the skillet. Cook for 5 minutes until vegetables are tender.
3. Stir in soy sauce, rice vinegar, and sesame oil. Cook for another 2 minutes.
4. Spoon the turkey mixture into lettuce leaves.
5. Serve immediately.

NUTRITIONAL INFORMATION (PER SERVING)

250 calories, 12g fat, 10g carbohydrates, 25g protein

PREP TIME

15Minutes

COOKING TIME

30 Minutes

SERVINGS

4

4) Quinoa and Black Bean Stuffed Peppers

A delicious and filling vegetarian dish that's rich in fiber and protein, perfect for any meal.

INGREDIENTS

- 4 bell peppers, tops cut off and seeds removed
- 1 cup quinoa
- 2 cups water or vegetable broth
- 1 can (15 oz) black beans, rinsed and drained
- 1 cup corn kernels (fresh or frozen)
- 1 cup diced tomatoes
- 1 teaspoon cumin
- 1 teaspoon chili powder
- 1/2 cup shredded cheese (optional)
- Salt and pepper to taste

PROCEDURE

1. Preheat the oven to 375°F (190°C).
2. Rinse the quinoa under cold water. In a medium saucepan, bring 2 cups of water or broth to a boil. Add the quinoa, reduce heat, cover, and simmer for 15 minutes or until the water is absorbed.
3. In a large bowl, combine the cooked quinoa, black beans, corn, diced tomatoes, cumin, chili powder, salt, and pepper.
4. Stuff each bell pepper with the quinoa mixture and place them in a baking dish.
5. If using, sprinkle shredded cheese on top of each stuffed pepper.
6. Cover with foil and bake for 25 minutes. Remove the foil and bake for an additional 5 minutes, or until the peppers are tender.
7. Serve hot.

NUTRITIONAL INFORMATION (PER SERVING)

250 calories, 12g fat, 10g carbohydrates, 25g protein

5) Chicken and Broccoli Stir-Fry

A quick and easy stir-fry that's packed with lean chicken and vibrant broccoli, perfect for a healthy dinner.

INGREDIENTS

- 1 lb boneless, skinless chicken breasts, sliced thinly
- 4 cups broccoli florets
- 1 red bell pepper, sliced
- 2 tablespoons olive oil
- 3 garlic cloves, minced
- 1/4 cup low-sodium soy sauce
- 1 tablespoon cornstarch
- 1/2 cup chicken broth
- 1 tablespoon hoisin sauce
- 1 teaspoon sesame oil
- Cooked brown rice (optional)

PROCEDURE

1. In a small bowl, whisk together soy sauce, cornstarch, chicken broth, hoisin sauce, and sesame oil.
2. In a large skillet or wok, heat olive oil over medium-high heat. Add chicken slices and cook until browned and cooked through, about 5-7 minutes. Remove chicken from skillet and set aside.
3. In the same skillet, add garlic, broccoli, and red bell pepper. Stir-fry for 5 minutes until vegetables are tender-crisp.
4. Return the chicken to the skillet. Pour the sauce over the chicken and vegetables. Cook for 2-3 minutes until the sauce thickens.
5. Serve immediately over cooked brown rice if desired.

NUTRITIONAL INFORMATION (PER SERVING)

250 calories, 12g fat, 10g carbohydrates, 25g protein

PREP TIME

10 Minutes

COOKING TIME

10 Minutes

SERVINGS

4

6) Zucchini Noodles

with Asparagus and Quinoa

A light, flavorful, and low-carb alternative to traditional pasta that is perfect for lunch or dinner.

INGREDIENTS

- 4 medium zucchinis, spiralized
- 1 cup cherry tomatoes, halved
- 1 cup basil pesto (store-bought or homemade)
- 2 tablespoons olive oil
- Salt and pepper to taste
- Grated Parmesan cheese (optional)

PROCEDURE

1. Heat olive oil in a large pan over medium heat.
2. Add spiralized zucchini and sauté for 3-4 minutes until slightly tender.
3. Add cherry tomatoes and cook for another 2 minutes.
4. Remove from heat and stir in basil pesto.
5. Season with salt and pepper.
6. Serve immediately, topped with grated Parmesan cheese if desired.

NUTRITIONAL INFORMATION (PER SERVING)

150 calories, 7g carbs, 13g fat, 4g protein

7)Lentil Soup
with Spinach and Carrots

A hearty and nutritious soup packed with protein and fiber, perfect for a comforting meal.

INGREDIENTS

- 1 cup dry lentils, rinsed
- 6 cups vegetable broth
- 1 onion, chopped
- 2 carrots, diced
- 2 celery stalks, diced
- 3 cups fresh spinach, chopped
- 2 garlic cloves, minced
- 1 teaspoon cumin
- 1 teaspoon thyme
- Salt and pepper to taste
- 2 tablespoons olive oil

PROCEDURE

1. Heat olive oil in a large pot over medium heat.
2. Add onions, carrots, and celery. Sauté for 5-7 minutes until softened.
3. Add garlic, cumin, and thyme. Cook for 1 minute until fragrant.
4. Stir in lentils and vegetable broth. Bring to a boil.
5. Reduce heat and simmer for 20-25 minutes until lentils are tender.
6. Add spinach and cook for another 5 minutes.
7. Season with salt and pepper before serving

NUTRITIONAL INFORMATION (PER SERVING)

150 calories, 7g carbs, 13g fat, 4g protein

PREP TIME

15 Minutes

COOKING TIME

10 Minutes

SERVINGS

4

8) Greek Salad
with Grilled Shrimp

A fresh and vibrant salad with juicy grilled shrimp, perfect for a light and satisfying meal.

INGREDIENTS

- 1 lb shrimp, peeled and deveined
- 1 cucumber, diced
- 1 pint cherry tomatoes, halved
- 1 red onion, thinly sliced
- 1 bell pepper, diced
- 1/2 cup Kalamata olives, pitted and sliced
- 4 oz feta cheese, crumbled
- 2 tablespoons olive oil
- 1 tablespoon red wine vinegar
- 1 teaspoon dried oregano
- Salt and pepper to taste

PROCEDURE

1. Preheat grill to medium-high heat.
2. Toss shrimp with 1 tablespoon olive oil, salt, and pepper. Grill for 2-3 minutes per side until pink and opaque.
3. In a large bowl, combine cucumber, cherry tomatoes, red onion, bell pepper, and olives.
4. Add grilled shrimp to the salad.
5. In a small bowl, whisk together remaining olive oil, red wine vinegar, oregano, salt, and pepper. Drizzle over salad.
6. Toss gently to combine and top with crumbled feta cheese.

NUTRITIONAL INFORMATION (PER SERVING)

250 calories, 10g carbs, 15g fat, 20g protein

9) Cauliflower Rice Bowl

with Grilled Chicken and Veggies

A low-carb, nutrient-dense bowl that is both delicious and satisfying.

INGREDIENTS

- 1 head cauliflower, riced
- 2 chicken breasts, grilled and sliced
- 1 red bell pepper, sliced
- 1 yellow bell pepper, sliced
- 1 zucchini, sliced
- 2 tablespoons olive oil
- 1 teaspoon garlic powder
- 1 teaspoon paprika
- Salt and pepper to taste

PROCEDURE

1. Preheat oven to 400°F (200°C).
2. Toss bell peppers and zucchini with olive oil, garlic powder, paprika, salt, and pepper. Spread on a baking sheet and roast for 15-20 minutes.
3. In a large pan, cook cauliflower rice over medium heat for 5-7 minutes until tender.
4. Divide cauliflower rice into bowls. Top with grilled chicken and roasted vegetables.
5. Serve immediately.

NUTRITIONAL INFORMATION (PER SERVING)

300 calories, 12g carbs, 15g fat, 30g protein

10) Turkey Chili
with Kidney Beans

A hearty and flavorful chili packed with lean protein and fiber, perfect for a cozy dinner.

INGREDIENTS

- 1 lb ground turkey
- 1 can (15 oz) kidney beans, drained and rinsed
- 1 can (15 oz) diced tomatoes
- 1 onion, chopped
- 2 garlic cloves, minced
- 1 red bell pepper, diced
- 2 tablespoons chili powder
- 1 teaspoon cumin
- 1 teaspoon paprika
- Salt and pepper to taste
- 2 tablespoons olive oil

PROCEDURE

1. Heat olive oil in a large pot over medium heat.
2. Add onion and bell pepper. Sauté for 5-7 minutes until softened.
3. Add garlic, chili powder, cumin, and paprika. Cook for 1 minute.
4. Add ground turkey and cook until browned.
5. Stir in kidney beans and diced tomatoes. Bring to a boil.
6. Reduce heat and simmer for 30 minutes. Season with salt and pepper before serving.

NUTRITIONAL INFORMATION (PER SERVING)

280 calories, 25g carbs, 10g fat, 25g protein

11)Grilled Portobello Mushrooms
with Quinoa Salad

A light yet satisfying meal, perfect for a healthy lunch or dinner. Grilled Portobello mushrooms pair beautifully with a zesty quinoa salad.

INGREDIENTS

- 4 large Portobello mushrooms, stems removed
- 1 cup quinoa
- 2 cups water
- 1 cup cherry tomatoes, halved
- 1 cucumber, diced
- 1/4 cup red onion, finely chopped
- 2 tablespoons olive oil
- 1 tablespoon balsamic vinegar
- 1 teaspoon dried oregano
- Salt and pepper to taste
- Fresh parsley for garnish

PROCEDURE

1. Preheat the grill to medium-high heat.
2. Cook quinoa according to package instructions. Fluff with a fork and let cool.
3. Brush mushrooms with 1 tablespoon olive oil and season with salt and pepper.
4. Grill mushrooms for 5-7 minutes on each side until tender.
5. In a large bowl, combine quinoa, cherry tomatoes, cucumber, and red onion.
6. In a small bowl, whisk together remaining olive oil, balsamic vinegar, oregano, salt, and pepper. Pour over quinoa salad and mix well.
7. Serve grilled mushrooms topped with quinoa salad. Garnish with fresh parsley.

NUTRITIONAL INFORMATION (PER SERVING)

230 calories, 10g fat, 28g carbohydrates, 7g protein

12) Spinach and Feta Stuffed

Chicken Breasts

Juicy chicken breasts stuffed with a flavorful mixture of spinach and feta, baked to perfection for a delicious and healthy meal.

INGREDIENTS

- 4 boneless, skinless chicken breasts
- 1 cup fresh spinach, chopped
- 1/2 cup feta cheese, crumbled
- 1 tablespoon olive oil
- 1 teaspoon garlic powder
- Salt and pepper to taste
- Toothpicks

PROCEDURE

1. Preheat oven to 375°F (190°C).
2. In a bowl, mix spinach, feta cheese, garlic powder, salt, and pepper.
3. Cut a pocket into each chicken breast and stuff with the spinach mixture.
4. Secure the opening with toothpicks.
5. Heat olive oil in an oven-safe skillet over medium-high heat. Sear chicken breasts for 3-4 minutes on each side until golden.
6. Transfer skillet to the oven and bake for 20-25 minutes, until chicken is cooked through.

NUTRITIONAL INFORMATION (PER SERVING)

290 calories, 12g fat, 2g carbohydrates, 43g protein

13) Broiled Tilapia
with Steamed Broccoli

A simple and quick recipe featuring tender broiled tilapia and nutritious steamed broccoli.

INGREDIENTS

- 4 tilapia fillets
- 2 tablespoons olive oil
- 1 teaspoon paprika
- 1 teaspoon garlic powder
- Salt and pepper to taste
- 1 large head broccoli, cut into florets
- 1 lemon, cut into wedges

PROCEDURE

1. Preheat broiler on high.
2. Place tilapia fillets on a baking sheet and brush with olive oil. Season with paprika, garlic powder, salt, and pepper.
3. Broil for 8-10 minutes, until fish flakes easily with a fork.
4. Meanwhile, steam broccoli florets until tender, about 5-7 minutes.
5. Serve tilapia with steamed broccoli and lemon wedges.

NUTRITIONAL INFORMATION (PER SERVING)

220 calories, 11g fat, 6g carbohydrates, 25g protein

14) Turkey Meatballs
with Zucchini Noodles

A healthier twist on spaghetti and meatballs, using lean turkey and zucchini noodles for a low-carb option.

INGREDIENTS

- 1 pound ground turkey
- 1/4 cup whole wheat breadcrumbs
- 1/4 cup grated Parmesan cheese
- 1 egg
- 2 cloves garlic, minced
- 1 teaspoon dried basil
- 1 teaspoon dried oregano
- Salt and pepper to taste
- 4 medium zucchinis, spiralized
- 1 tablespoon olive oil
- 1 cup marinara sauce

PROCEDURE

1. Preheat oven to 375°F (190°C).
2. In a large bowl, combine ground turkey, breadcrumbs, Parmesan cheese, egg, garlic, basil, oregano, salt, and pepper. Mix well and form into meatballs.
3. Place meatballs on a baking sheet and bake for 20-25 minutes, until cooked through.
4. In a large skillet, heat olive oil over medium heat. Add zucchini noodles and sauté for 3-4 minutes until tender.
5. Heat marinara sauce in a small saucepan.
6. Serve meatballs over zucchini noodles, topped with marinara sauce.

NUTRITIONAL INFORMATION (PER SERVING)

280 calories, 14g fat, 11g carbohydrates, 28g protein

15) Baked Cod

with Roasted Brussels Sprouts

An easy and nutritious meal featuring flaky baked cod and crispy roasted Brussels sprouts.

INGREDIENTS

- 4 cod fillets
- 1 tablespoon olive oil
- 1 teaspoon lemon zest
- 1 teaspoon dried thyme
- Salt and pepper to taste
- 1 pound Brussels sprouts, halved
- 2 tablespoons balsamic vinegar

PROCEDURE

1. Preheat oven to 400°F (200°C).
2. Place Brussels sprouts on a baking sheet, drizzle with olive oil, balsamic vinegar, salt, and pepper. Toss to coat.
3. Roast Brussels sprouts for 15 minutes.
4. Place cod fillets on a separate baking sheet. Drizzle with olive oil, sprinkle with lemon zest, thyme, salt, and pepper.
5. Bake cod alongside Brussels sprouts for another 10-12 minutes, until fish is cooked through and Brussels sprouts are crispy.

NUTRITIONAL INFORMATION (PER SERVING)

250 calories, 10g fat, 15g carbohydrates, 25g protein

16) Chicken and Avocado Salad

A fresh and filling salad with grilled chicken, creamy avocado, and a tangy lime dressing.

INGREDIENTS

- 2 boneless, skinless chicken breasts
- 1 tablespoon olive oil
- 1 teaspoon paprika
- Salt and pepper to taste
- 1 large avocado, diced
- 4 cups mixed greens
- 1 cup cherry tomatoes, halved
- 1/4 cup red onion, sliced
- Juice of 1 lime
- 1 tablespoon olive oil
- 1 teaspoon honey
- Salt and pepper to taste

PROCEDURE

1. Preheat grill to medium-high heat.
2. Brush chicken breasts with olive oil, season with paprika, salt, and pepper. Grill for 5-6 minutes on each side until cooked through. Let rest and then slice.
3. In a large bowl, combine mixed greens, avocado, cherry tomatoes, and red onion.
4. In a small bowl, whisk together lime juice, olive oil, honey, salt, and pepper. Drizzle over salad and toss to coat.
5. Top salad with sliced chicken.

NUTRITIONAL INFORMATION (PER SERVING)

250 calories, 10g fat, 15g carbohydrates, 25g protein

17) Vegetable and Tofu Stir-Fry

A quick and vibrant stir-fry packed with colorful vegetables and protein-rich tofu.

INGREDIENTS

- 1 block firm tofu, cubed
- 2 tablespoons soy sauce (low sodium)
- 1 tablespoon sesame oil
- 1 red bell pepper, sliced
- 1 yellow bell pepper, sliced
- 1 cup broccoli florets
- 1 carrot, julienned
- 2 cloves garlic, minced
- 1 tablespoon fresh ginger, grated
- 2 green onions, chopped
- 1 tablespoon sesame seeds

PROCEDURE

1. In a bowl, marinate tofu cubes in soy sauce for 10 minutes.
2. Heat sesame oil in a large skillet or wok over medium-high heat. Add tofu and cook until golden brown, about 5-7 minutes. Remove and set aside.
3. In the same skillet, add garlic, ginger, and all vegetables. Stir-fry for 5-7 minutes until tender.
4. Return tofu to the skillet, toss to combine, and heat through.
5. Sprinkle with green onions and sesame seeds before serving.

NUTRITIONAL INFORMATION (PER SERVING)

220 calories, 14g fat, 14g carbohydrates, 12g protein

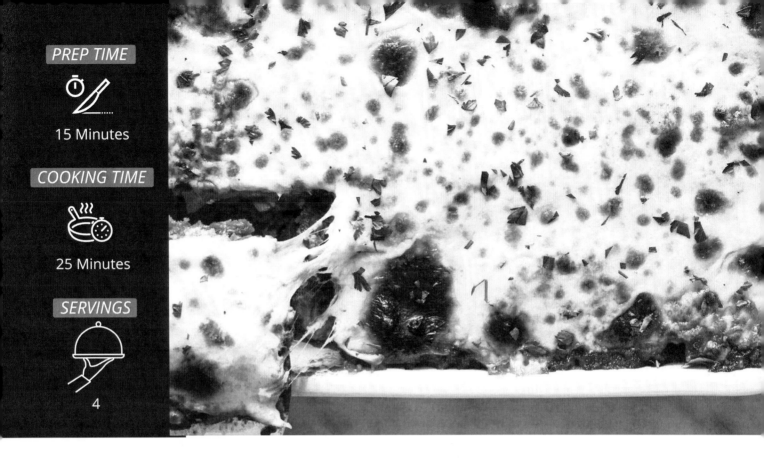

18) Eggplant Parmesan (Baked)

A lighter version of the classic dish, baked instead of fried, perfect for a hearty meal.

INGREDIENTS

- 2 large eggplants, sliced into rounds
- 1 cup whole wheat breadcrumbs
- 1/2 cup grated Parmesan cheese
- 2 eggs, beaten
- 2 cups marinara sauce
- 1 cup shredded mozzarella cheese
- Fresh basil for garnish

PROCEDURE

1. Preheat oven to 375°F (190°C).
2. Dip eggplant slices in beaten eggs, then coat with a mixture of breadcrumbs and Parmesan cheese.
3. Place on a baking sheet and bake for 20 minutes, turning halfway through.
4. Spread a thin layer of marinara sauce in a baking dish. Layer with eggplant slices, more marinara sauce, and mozzarella cheese. Repeat layers.
5. Bake for an additional 10 minutes, until cheese is melted and bubbly.
6. Garnish with fresh basil before serving.

NUTRITIONAL INFORMATION (PER SERVING)

300 calories, 15g fat, 32g carbohydrates, 12g protein

19) Cabbage Rolls

with Ground Turkey and Brown Rice

Savory cabbage rolls stuffed with lean ground turkey and nutritious brown rice, simmered in a rich tomato sauce.

INGREDIENTS

- 1 head green cabbage
- 1 pound ground turkey
- 1 cup cooked brown rice
- 1 onion, finely chopped
- 2 cloves garlic, minced
- 1 teaspoon dried thyme
- Salt and pepper to taste
- 2 cups tomato sauce
- 1 tablespoon olive oil

PROCEDURE

1. Preheat oven to 350°F (175°C).
2. Bring a large pot of water to a boil. Carefully remove leaves from cabbage and blanch in boiling water for 2-3 minutes until softened.
3. In a bowl, combine ground turkey, brown rice, onion, garlic, thyme, salt, and pepper.
4. Place a portion of the turkey mixture in the center of each cabbage leaf. Roll up and place seam-side down in a baking dish.
5. Pour tomato sauce over cabbage rolls and drizzle with olive oil.
6. Cover with foil and bake for 1 hour.

NUTRITIONAL INFORMATION (PER SERVING)

340 calories, 12g fat, 30g carbohydrates, 28g protein

20) Beef and Vegetable Kebabs
with Quinoa

Flavorful beef and vegetable skewers served over fluffy quinoa, perfect for a summer cookout.

INGREDIENTS

- 1 pound beef sirloin, cut into cubes
- 1 red bell pepper, cut into squares
- 1 yellow bell pepper, cut into squares
- 1 red onion, cut into wedges
- 1 zucchini, sliced
- 2 tablespoons olive oil
- 1 tablespoon soy sauce (low sodium)
- 1 teaspoon garlic powder
- Salt and pepper to taste
- 1 cup quinoa
- 2 cups water

PROCEDURE

1. Preheat grill to medium-high heat.
2. Thread beef, bell peppers, onion, and zucchini onto skewers. Brush with olive oil and season with soy sauce, garlic powder, salt, and pepper.
3. Grill kebabs for 10-15 minutes, turning occasionally, until beef is cooked to desired doneness.
4. Meanwhile, cook quinoa according to package instructions.
5. Serve kebabs over a bed of quinoa.

NUTRITIONAL INFORMATION (PER SERVING)

350 calories, 15g fat, 30g carbohydrates, 28g protein

21) Chickpea and Spinach Stew

This hearty and nutritious stew is perfect for a quick lunch or dinner. It's packed with protein and fiber, making it ideal for maintaining blood sugar levels.

INGREDIENTS

- 1 tablespoon olive oil
- 1 onion, chopped
- 2 garlic cloves, minced
- 1 can (15 oz) chickpeas, drained and rinsed
- 1 can (14.5 oz) diced tomatoes
- 4 cups fresh spinach
- 1 teaspoon ground cumin
- 1 teaspoon ground coriander
- 1 teaspoon paprika
- Salt and pepper to taste

PROCEDURE

1. Heat the olive oil in a large pot over medium heat.
2. Add the onion and garlic, cooking until softened, about 5 minutes.
3. Stir in the chickpeas, diced tomatoes, cumin, coriander, and paprika. Simmer for 15 minutes.
4. Add the spinach and cook until wilted, about 5 minutes.
5. Season with salt and pepper to taste. Serve warm.

NUTRITIONAL INFORMATION (PER SERVING)

220 calories, 8g protein, 35g carbs, 6g fat

PREP TIME

5 Minutes

COOKING TIME

10 Minutes

SERVINGS

4

22) Grilled Salmon Tacos

with Cabbage Slaw

These flavorful salmon tacos are a quick and healthy dinner option, perfect for a light but satisfying meal.

INGREDIENTS

- 4 salmon fillets
- 1 tablespoon olive oil
- 1 teaspoon cumin
- 1 teaspoon chili powder
- Salt and pepper to taste
- 8 small corn tortillas
- 2 cups shredded cabbage
- 1/4 cup chopped cilantro
- Juice of 1 lime

PROCEDURE

1. Preheat the grill to medium-high heat.
2. Rub the salmon fillets with olive oil, cumin, chili powder, salt, and pepper.
3. Grill the salmon for 4-5 minutes per side, until cooked through.
4. In a bowl, toss the shredded cabbage with cilantro and lime juice.
5. Warm the tortillas on the grill for about 30 seconds per side.
6. Assemble the tacos by placing a piece of salmon in each tortilla and topping with the cabbage slaw. Serve immediately.

NUTRITIONAL INFORMATION (PER SERVING)

300 calories, 25g protein, 20g carbs, 15g fat

23) Turkey and Spinach Stuffed Bell Peppers

These stuffed bell peppers are a delicious and nutrient-packed option for dinner, perfect for keeping your blood sugar in check.

INGREDIENTS

- 4 large bell peppers, tops cut off and seeds removed
- 1 tablespoon olive oil
- 1 onion, chopped
- 2 garlic cloves, minced
- 1 pound ground turkey
- 2 cups fresh spinach, chopped
- 1 cup cooked quinoa
- 1 teaspoon dried oregano
- Salt and pepper to taste
- 1/2 cup shredded mozzarella cheese (optional)

PROCEDURE

1. Preheat the oven to 375°F (190°C).
2. In a large skillet, heat the olive oil over medium heat. Add the onion and garlic, cooking until softened, about 5 minutes.
3. Add the ground turkey and cook until browned, about 7-10 minutes.
4. Stir in the spinach, quinoa, oregano, salt, and pepper. Cook until the spinach is wilted, about 3 minutes.
5. Stuff the bell peppers with the turkey mixture and place in a baking dish.
6. Top with shredded mozzarella cheese, if using.
7. Bake for 25-30 minutes, until the peppers are tender and the cheese is melted and bubbly.

NUTRITIONAL INFORMATION (PER SERVING)

320 calories, 30g protein, 25g carbs, 10g fat

65

24) Chicken Fajita Bowl
with Cauliflower Rice

This chicken fajita bowl is a low-carb delight, full of vibrant flavors and perfect for a diabetic-friendly meal.

INGREDIENTS

- 1 tablespoon olive oil
- 1 pound chicken breast, sliced into strips
- 1 red bell pepper, sliced
- 1 green bell pepper, sliced
- 1 onion, sliced
- 2 teaspoons fajita seasoning
- 1 head cauliflower, riced
- 1 avocado, sliced
- Fresh cilantro, chopped (for garnish)

PROCEDURE

1. Heat olive oil in a large skillet over medium-high heat.
2. Add the chicken strips and cook until browned, about 5-7 minutes.
3. Add the bell peppers and onion, cooking until tender, about 5 minutes.
4. Stir in the fajita seasoning and cook for another 2 minutes.
5. In a separate skillet, sauté the riced cauliflower over medium heat until tender, about 5 minutes.
6. Serve the chicken and veggies over the cauliflower rice. Top with avocado slices and fresh cilantro.

NUTRITIONAL INFORMATION (PER SERVING)

350 calories, 35g protein, 20g carbs, 15g fat

PREP TIME

15 Minutes

COOKING TIME

20 Minutes

SERVINGS

4

25) Seared Tuna Salad

with Avocado and Mixed Greens

This fresh and vibrant seared tuna salad is full of healthy fats and protein, making it an ideal choice for a light and nutritious meal.

INGREDIENTS

- 4 tuna steaks
- 1 tablespoon olive oil
- Salt and pepper to taste
- 6 cups mixed greens
- 1 avocado, sliced
- 1 cup cherry tomatoes, halved
- 1/4 cup red onion, thinly sliced
- Juice of 1 lemon
- 2 tablespoons olive oil (for dressing)

PROCEDURE

1. Heat 1 tablespoon olive oil in a skillet over medium-high heat.
2. Season the tuna steaks with salt and pepper. Sear the tuna for 2-3 minutes per side, until desired doneness. Let rest for 5 minutes, then slice.
3. In a large bowl, combine the mixed greens, avocado, cherry tomatoes, and red onion.
4. Drizzle with lemon juice and 2 tablespoons olive oil. Toss to combine.
5. Top the salad with the seared tuna slices. Serve immediately.

NUTRITIONAL INFORMATION (PER SERVING)

350 calories, 35g protein, 15g carbs, 18g fat

26) Vegetable and Lentil Curry

This warm and comforting vegetable and lentil curry is packed with protein and fiber, making it a great option for a diabetic-friendly dinner.

INGREDIENTS

- 1 tablespoon olive oil
- 1 onion, chopped
- 2 garlic cloves, minced
- 1 tablespoon ginger, grated
- 1 cup dried lentils, rinsed
- 1 can (14.5 oz) diced tomatoes
- 2 cups vegetable broth
- 1 cup coconut milk
- 2 cups mixed vegetables (carrots, peas, green beans)
- 2 teaspoons curry powder
- Salt and pepper to taste
- Fresh cilantro (for garnish)

PROCEDURE

1. Heat the olive oil in a large pot over medium heat.
2. Add the onion, garlic, and ginger, cooking until softened, about 5 minutes.
3. Stir in the lentils, diced tomatoes, vegetable broth, coconut milk, and curry powder. Bring to a boil.
4. Reduce heat and simmer for 20 minutes, until the lentils are tender.
5. Add the mixed vegetables and cook for another 10 minutes.
6. Season with salt and pepper to taste. Garnish with fresh cilantro and serve.

NUTRITIONAL INFORMATION (PER SERVING)

400 calories, 15g protein, 45g carbs, 18g fat

27) Garlic Shrimp

with Zoodles (Zucchini Noodles)

This garlic shrimp with zoodles is a light, low-carb dish that's perfect for a quick and healthy dinner.

INGREDIENTS

- 1 tablespoon olive oil
- 1 pound shrimp, peeled and deveined
- 3 garlic cloves, minced
- 4 large zucchinis, spiralized
- 1/4 teaspoon red pepper flakes
- Juice of 1 lemon
- Salt and pepper to taste
- Fresh parsley, chopped (for garnish)

PROCEDURE

1. Heat the olive oil in a large skillet over medium heat.
2. Add the shrimp and garlic, cooking until the shrimp are pink and opaque, about 3-4 minutes.
3. Add the spiralized zucchini noodles (zoodles) and red pepper flakes to the skillet. Cook for another 2-3 minutes, until the zoodles are tender.
4. Stir in the lemon juice and season with salt and pepper to taste.
5. Garnish with fresh parsley and serve immediately.

NUTRITIONAL INFORMATION (PER SERVING)

250 calories, 30g protein, 10g carbs, 10g fat

28) Spinach and Mushroom
Stuffed Pork Tenderloin

This elegant stuffed pork tenderloin is filled with nutritious spinach and mushrooms, making it a perfect diabetic-friendly dinner option.

INGREDIENTS

- 1 pork tenderloin (about 1.5 pounds)
- 1 tablespoon olive oil
- 1 onion, chopped
- 2 garlic cloves, minced
- 2 cups fresh spinach, chopped
- 1 cup mushrooms, chopped
- 1 teaspoon dried thyme
- Salt and pepper to taste

PROCEDURE

1. Preheat the oven to 375°F (190°C).
2. In a skillet, heat the olive oil over medium heat. Add the onion and garlic, cooking until softened, about 5 minutes.
3. Add the spinach, mushrooms, and thyme, cooking until the spinach is wilted and the mushrooms are tender, about 5 minutes. Season with salt and pepper.
4. Cut a lengthwise slit down the center of the pork tenderloin, being careful not to cut all the way through. Open the tenderloin like a book and spread the spinach and mushroom mixture evenly inside.
5. Roll up the tenderloin and secure with kitchen twine.
6. Place the tenderloin in a baking dish and roast for 30-35 minutes, until the internal temperature reaches 145°F (63°C).
7. Let rest for 5 minutes before slicing and serving.

NUTRITIONAL INFORMATION (PER SERVING)

250 calories, 30g protein, 10g carbs, 10g fat

29)Baked Eggplant
with Tomato and Mozzarella

This baked eggplant dish is a delicious, low-carb option that's perfect for a light dinner or lunch, featuring the classic combination of tomato and mozzarella.

INGREDIENTS

- 2 large eggplants, sliced into rounds
- 1 tablespoon olive oil
- 1 can (14.5 oz) diced tomatoes
- 2 garlic cloves, minced
- 1 teaspoon dried basil
- 1/2 teaspoon dried oregano
- Salt and pepper to taste
- 1 cup shredded mozzarella cheese
- Fresh basil leaves (for garnish)

PROCEDURE

1. Preheat the oven to 375°F (190°C).
2. Arrange the eggplant slices on a baking sheet and brush with olive oil. Bake for 15 minutes, until tender.
3. In a saucepan, combine the diced tomatoes, garlic, dried basil, oregano, salt, and pepper. Simmer for 10 minutes.
4. Arrange the baked eggplant slices in a baking dish. Spoon the tomato mixture over the eggplant.
5. Sprinkle the mozzarella cheese on top.
6. Bake for another 15 minutes, until the cheese is melted and bubbly.
7. Garnish with fresh basil leaves and serve.

NUTRITIONAL INFORMATION (PER SERVING)

280 calories, 12g protein, 20g carbs, 18g fat

71

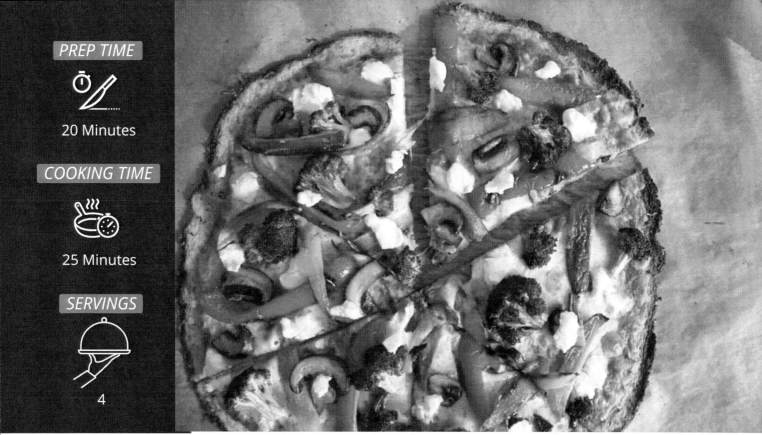

30) Cauliflower Crust Pizza

with Veggie Toppings

Enjoy a pizza night with this healthy cauliflower crust pizza, loaded with fresh veggies and perfect for a diabetic-friendly meal.

INGREDIENTS

- 1 large head cauliflower, riced
- 1 cup shredded mozzarella cheese
- 1/4 cup grated Parmesan cheese
- 1 egg, beaten
- 1 teaspoon dried oregano
- Salt and pepper to taste
- 1/2 cup tomato sauce
- 1 cup mixed vegetables (bell peppers, onions, mushrooms), sliced
- 1 cup shredded mozzarella cheese (for topping)

PROCEDURE

1. Preheat the oven to 400°F (200°C).
2. Microwave the riced cauliflower for 5 minutes, until soft. Let cool, then squeeze out excess moisture using a clean towel.
3. In a bowl, combine the cauliflower, 1 cup mozzarella, Parmesan, egg, oregano, salt, and pepper. Mix well.
4. Press the mixture onto a parchment-lined baking sheet to form a crust. Bake for 15 minutes, until golden and firm.
5. Spread the tomato sauce over the crust. Top with mixed vegetables and the remaining 1 cup mozzarella cheese.
6. Bake for another 10 minutes, until the cheese is melted and bubbly. Serve hot.

NUTRITIONAL INFORMATION (PER SERVING)

300 calories, 20g protein, 15g carbs, 18g fat

HEALTHY SNACKS
RECIPES

1) Celery Sticks
with Almond Butter

A crunchy and satisfying snack that's packed with fiber and healthy fats.

INGREDIENTS

- 2 celery stalks
- 2 tablespoons almond butter

PROCEDURE

1. Wash and trim the celery stalks.
2. Cut the celery into sticks.
3. Spread almond butter into the groove of each celery stick.
4. Serve immediately.

NUTRITIONAL INFORMATION (PER SERVING)

Calories: 190, Carbs: 6g, Protein: 5g, Fat: 17g

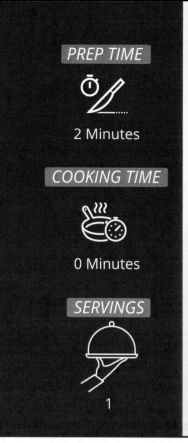

2) Greek Yogurt
with a Sprinkle of Chia Seeds

A creamy and nutritious snack that's rich in protein and omega-3 fatty acids.

INGREDIENTS

- 1 cup plain Greek yogurt
- 1 tablespoon chia seeds

PROCEDURE

1. Spoon the Greek yogurt into a bowl.
2. Sprinkle chia seeds on top.
3. Stir to combine and enjoy.

NUTRITIONAL INFORMATION (PER SERVING)

Calories: 150, Carbs: 8g, Protein: 15g, Fat: 6g

PREP TIME

2 Minutes

COOKING TIME

0 Minutes

SERVINGS

1

3) **Apple Slices**
with Peanut Butter

A sweet and savory snack that's perfect for a quick energy boost.

INGREDIENTS

- 1 medium apple
- 2 tablespoons peanut butter

PROCEDURE

1. Wash and core the apple.
2. Slice the apple into wedges.
3. Dip each apple slice into peanut butter.
4. Serve immediately.

NUTRITIONAL INFORMATION (PER SERVING)

Calories: 210, Carbs: 22g, Protein: 4g, Fat: 12g

4) Mixed Nuts (Unsalted)

A simple and portable snack that provides a mix of healthy fats and protein.

INGREDIENTS

- 1/4 cup mixed nuts (unsalted)

PROCEDURE

1. Measure out 1/4 cup of mixed nuts.
2. Place in a small bowl or container for easy snacking.

NUTRITIONAL INFORMATION (PER SERVING)

Calories: 200, Carbs: 6g, Protein: 6g, Fat: 18g

5) Cucumber Slices with Hummus

A light and refreshing snack that's full of fiber and plant-based protein.

INGREDIENTS

- 1 cucumber
- 1/4 cup hummus

PROCEDURE

1. Wash and peel the cucumber.
2. Slice the cucumber into rounds.
3. Serve with hummus on the side for dipping.

NUTRITIONAL INFORMATION (PER SERVING)

Calories: 130, Carbs: 14g, Protein: 4g, Fat: 6g

6) Carrot Sticks
with Guacamole

A colorful and nutritious snack that's rich in vitamins and healthy fats.

INGREDIENTS

- 2 large carrots
- 1/4 cup guacamole

PROCEDURE

1. Wash and peel the carrots.
2. Cut the carrots into sticks.
3. Serve with guacamole on the side for dipping.

NUTRITIONAL INFORMATION (PER SERVING)

Calories: 150, Carbs: 15g, Protein: 2g, Fat: 10g

7) Hard-Boiled Eggs

A protein-packed snack that's easy to prepare and perfect for on-the-go.

INGREDIENTS

- 2 large eggs

PROCEDURE

1. Place the eggs in a pot and cover with water.
2. Bring to a boil, then reduce heat and simmer for 10 minutes.
3. Remove from heat, cool under cold running water, and peel.
4. Serve immediately or store in the refrigerator.

NUTRITIONAL INFORMATION (PER SERVING)

Calories: 140, Carbs: 1g, Protein: 12g, Fat: 10g

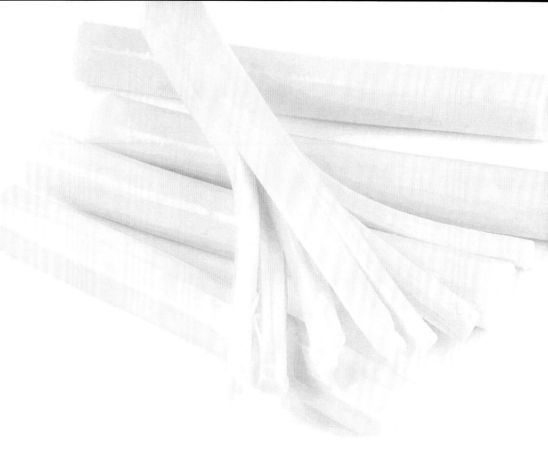

8) String Cheese

A convenient and calcium-rich snack that's great for any time of day.

INGREDIENTS

- 1 stick of string cheese

PROCEDURE

1. Simply unwrap and enjoy!

NUTRITIONAL INFORMATION (PER SERVING)

Calories: 80, Carbs: 1g, Protein: 7g, Fat: 6g

9) Cherry Tomatoes and Mozzarella Balls

A tasty and colorful snack that's full of antioxidants and protein.

INGREDIENTS

- 1 cup cherry tomatoes
- 1/4 cup mozzarella balls

PROCEDURE

1. Wash the cherry tomatoes.
2. Combine cherry tomatoes and mozzarella balls in a bowl.
3. Serve immediately.

NUTRITIONAL INFORMATION (PER SERVING)

Calories: 150, Carbs: 6g, Protein: 9g, Fat: 10g

10) Berries with Cottage Cheese

A sweet and creamy snack that's rich in protein and antioxidants.

INGREDIENTS

- 1/2 cup mixed berries (strawberries, blueberries, raspberries)
- 1/2 cup cottage cheese

PROCEDURE

1. Wash and dry the berries.
2. Spoon cottage cheese into a bowl.
3. Top with mixed berries and enjoy.

NUTRITIONAL INFORMATION (PER SERVING)

Calories: 120, Carbs: 12g, Protein: 10g, Fat: 4g

11) Edamame (Steamed)

A simple and nutritious snack that is packed with protein and fiber. Perfect for a quick, satisfying bite.

INGREDIENTS

- 1 cup edamame (fresh or frozen)
- 1/2 teaspoon sea salt

PROCEDURE

1. Bring a pot of water to a boil.
2. Add the edamame and cook for 5 minutes until tender.
3. Drain and sprinkle with sea salt.
4. Serve warm or cold.

NUTRITIONAL INFORMATION (PER SERVING)

90 calories, 8g protein, 7g carbs, 4g fat

12) Sliced Bell Peppers
with Tzatziki Sauce

Colorful bell peppers paired with creamy tzatziki make a refreshing and healthy snack.

INGREDIENTS

- 1 red bell pepper, sliced
- 1 yellow bell pepper, sliced
- 1/2 cup tzatziki sauce (store-bought or homemade)

PROCEDURE

1. Wash and slice the bell peppers into strips.
2. Arrange the slices on a plate with a bowl of tzatziki sauce in the center.
3. Dip the bell pepper slices into the tzatziki sauce and enjoy.

NUTRITIONAL INFORMATION (PER SERVING)

80 calories, 2g protein, 10g carbs, 4g fat

PREP TIME

10 Minutes

COOKING TIME

15 Minutes

SERVINGS

4

13) Almond Flour Crackers
with Cheese

A crunchy and savory snack that is low in carbs and perfect for munching.

INGREDIENTS

- 1 cup almond flour
- 1 tablespoon olive oil
- 1/2 teaspoon sea salt
- 1/4 teaspoon garlic powder
- 1/4 cup water
- 4 ounces cheese, sliced

PROCEDURE

1. Preheat the oven to 350°F (175°C).
2. In a bowl, mix almond flour, olive oil, sea salt, and garlic powder.
3. Add water and mix until dough forms.
4. Roll out the dough between two sheets of parchment paper.
5. Cut into squares and place on a baking sheet.
6. Bake for 12-15 minutes until golden brown.
7. Serve with cheese slices.

NUTRITIONAL INFORMATION (PER SERVING)

150 calories, 6g protein, 4g carbs, 13g fat

14) Sliced Avocado
with Lime and Sea Salt

Creamy avocado seasoned simply with lime and sea salt for a quick and nutritious snack.

INGREDIENTS

- 1 ripe avocado
- 1 lime
- 1/4 teaspoon sea salt

PROCEDURE

1. Slice the avocado in half, remove the pit, and scoop out the flesh.
2. Slice the avocado and arrange on a plate.
3. Squeeze lime juice over the avocado slices and sprinkle with sea salt.

NUTRITIONAL INFORMATION (PER SERVING)

120 calories, 2g protein, 6g carbs, 11g fat

15) Kale Chips

A crispy and nutritious alternative to potato chips.

INGREDIENTS

- 1 bunch kale
- 1 tablespoon olive oil
- 1/2 teaspoon sea salt

PROCEDURE

1. Preheat the oven to 300°F (150°C).
2. Wash and dry the kale, removing the stems and tearing into pieces.
3. Toss the kale with olive oil and sea salt.
4. Spread on a baking sheet and bake for 15 minutes until crispy.

NUTRITIONAL INFORMATION (PER SERVING)

50 calories, 2g protein, 7g carbs, 2g fat

16) Turkey and Cheese Roll-Ups

A protein-packed snack that's easy to make and perfect for on-the-go.

INGREDIENTS

- 4 slices of turkey breast
- 4 slices of cheese (your choice)

PROCEDURE

1. Lay out a slice of turkey breast.
2. Place a slice of cheese on top.
3. Roll up the turkey and cheese together.
4. Repeat with the remaining slices.

NUTRITIONAL INFORMATION (PER SERVING)

100 calories, 10g protein, 1g carbs, 6g fat

17) Olives and Feta Cheese

A Mediterranean-inspired snack that's rich in healthy fats and flavor.

INGREDIENTS

- 1/2 cup mixed olives
- 1/4 cup feta cheese, cubed

PROCEDURE

1. Arrange olives and feta cheese cubes on a plate.
2. Serve as a simple and savory snack.

NUTRITIONAL INFORMATION (PER SERVING)

120 calories, 3g protein, 2g carbs, 11g fat

18) Chia Pudding
with Unsweetened Almond Milk

A delicious and nutritious pudding that's perfect for breakfast or a snack.

INGREDIENTS

- 1/4 cup chia seeds
- 1 cup unsweetened almond milk
- 1/2 teaspoon vanilla extract (optional)
- 1 teaspoon sweetener of your choice (optional)

PROCEDURE

1. In a bowl, mix chia seeds and almond milk.
2. Add vanilla extract and sweetener if using.
3. Stir well and refrigerate for at least 2 hours, stirring occasionally.
4. Serve chilled.

NUTRITIONAL INFORMATION (PER SERVING)

100 calories, 4g protein, 12g carbs, 5g fat

19) Pumpkin Seeds

A crunchy and nutrient-dense snack that's perfect for any time of day.

INGREDIENTS

- 1/2 cup pumpkin seeds
- 1/4 teaspoon sea salt

PROCEDURE

1. Place pumpkin seeds in a bowl.
2. Sprinkle with sea salt and mix well.
3. Enjoy as a quick and healthy snack.

NUTRITIONAL INFORMATION (PER SERVING)

90 calories, 5g protein, 4g carbs, 7g fat

20) Blueberries and Walnuts

A simple and nutritious combination that's rich in antioxidants and healthy fats.

INGREDIENTS

- 1 cup fresh blueberries
- 1/2 cup walnuts

PROCEDURE

1. Place blueberries and walnuts in a bowl.
2. Mix together and serve as a healthy snack.

NUTRITIONAL INFORMATION (PER SERVING)

150 calories, 3g protein, 15g carbs, 10g fat

PREP TIME

10 minutes

COOKING TIME

0 minutes

SERVINGS

4

21) Zucchini Slices
with Goat Cheese

A light and refreshing snack that's perfect for summer afternoons.

INGREDIENTS

- 2 medium zucchinis, thinly sliced
- 4 oz goat cheese
- 1 tbsp olive oil
- Salt and pepper to taste
- Fresh basil leaves, chopped (optional)

PROCEDURE

1. Arrange the zucchini slices on a platter.
2. Spread a small amount of goat cheese on each slice.
3. Drizzle with olive oil and season with salt and pepper.
4. Garnish with fresh basil leaves, if desired.

NUTRITIONAL INFORMATION (PER SERVING)

Calories: 110, Carbs: 4g, Protein: 6g, Fat: 9g

22) Radishes
with Herb Dip

A crunchy and flavorful snack, perfect for a quick bite.

INGREDIENTS

- 1 bunch radishes, trimmed and halved
- 1/2 cup Greek yogurt
- 1 tbsp fresh dill, chopped
- 1 tbsp fresh parsley, chopped
- 1 tsp lemon juice
- Salt and pepper to taste

PROCEDURE

1. In a bowl, mix the Greek yogurt, dill, parsley, lemon juice, salt, and pepper.
2. Serve the radishes with the herb dip.

NUTRITIONAL INFORMATION (PER SERVING)

Calories: 45, Carbs: 4g, Protein: 3g, Fat: 2g

PREP TIME

5 minutes

COOKING TIME

0 minutes

SERVINGS

1

23) Greek Yogurt
with Flaxseeds

A protein-packed snack to keep you full and energized.

INGREDIENTS

- 1 cup Greek yogurt
- 1 tbsp flaxseeds
- 1 tsp honey (optional)
- 1/2 tsp cinnamon (optional)

PROCEDURE

1. Scoop the Greek yogurt into a bowl.
2. Sprinkle with flaxseeds, honey, and cinnamon, if using.
3. Mix well and enjoy.

NUTRITIONAL INFORMATION (PER SERVING)

Calories: 150, Carbs: 10g, Protein: 14g, Fat: 5g

24)Homemade Trail Mix
(Nuts and Seeds)

A customizable and portable snack for any time of the day.

INGREDIENTS

- 1/2 cup almonds
- 1/2 cup walnuts
- 1/4 cup pumpkin seeds
- 1/4 cup sunflower seeds
- 1/4 cup unsweetened dried cranberries

PROCEDURE

1. Mix all ingredients in a bowl.
2. Store in an airtight container.

NUTRITIONAL INFORMATION (PER SERVING)

Calories: 200, Carbs: 8g, Protein: 6g, Fat: 17g

25)Bell Pepper and Cucumber Slices
with Salsa

A colorful and crunchy snack that's full of vitamins.

INGREDIENTS

- 2 bell peppers, sliced
- 1 cucumber, sliced
- 1 cup fresh salsa

PROCEDURE

1. Arrange the bell pepper and cucumber slices on a platter.
2. Serve with fresh salsa on the side.

NUTRITIONAL INFORMATION (PER SERVING)

Calories: 35, Carbs: 8g, Protein: 1g, Fat: 0g

26) Baked Apple Chips

A sweet and crunchy treat without added sugar.

INGREDIENTS

- 2 apples, thinly sliced
- 1/2 tsp cinnamon

PROCEDURE

1. Preheat the oven to 225°F (110°C).
2. Arrange the apple slices on a baking sheet lined with parchment paper.
3. Sprinkle with cinnamon.
4. Bake for 1 hour, flipping halfway through, until crisp.

NUTRITIONAL INFORMATION (PER SERVING)

Calories: 50, Carbs: 13g, Protein: 0g, Fat: 0g

PREP TIME

15 minutes

COOKING TIME

0 Minutes

SERVINGS

12 balls

27) Homemade Protein Balls

with Oats and Almond Butter

A delicious and nutritious snack that's easy to make ahead.

INGREDIENTS

- 1 cup rolled oats
- 1/2 cup almond butter
- 1/4 cup honey
- 1/4 cup flaxseeds
- 1/4 cup dark chocolate chips (optional)

PROCEDURE

1. In a bowl, mix all the ingredients until well combined.
2. Roll the mixture into 1-inch balls.
3. Refrigerate for at least 30 minutes before serving.

NUTRITIONAL INFORMATION (PER SERVING)

Calories: 100, Carbs: 12g, Protein: 3g, Fat: 5g

28) Sunflower Seeds

A simple, crunchy snack full of healthy fats and protein.

INGREDIENTS

- 1/4 cup unsalted sunflower seeds

PROCEDURE

1. Enjoy the sunflower seeds as a quick snack.

NUTRITIONAL INFORMATION (PER SERVING)

Calories: 190, Carbs: 6g, Protein: 6g, Fat: 16g

29) Seaweed Snacks

A savory and crispy snack that's low in calories.

INGREDIENTS

- 1 pack roasted seaweed snacks

PROCEDURE

1. Open the pack and enjoy.

NUTRITIONAL INFORMATION (PER SERVING)

Calories: 25, Carbs: 1g, Protein: 1g, Fat: 2g

PREP TIME

5 minutes

COOKING TIME

0 Minutes

SERVINGS

2

30) Low-Sugar Smoothie
with Spinach and Berries

A refreshing and nutritious smoothie that's perfect for any time of day.

INGREDIENTS

- 1 cup fresh spinach
- 1 cup mixed berries (strawberries, blueberries, raspberries)
- 1 cup unsweetened almond milk
- 1/2 banana
- 1 tbsp chia seeds

PROCEDURE

1. Blend all the ingredients until smooth.
2. Pour into glasses and enjoy immediately.

NUTRITIONAL INFORMATION (PER SERVING)

Calories: 25, Carbs: 1g, Protein: 1g, Fat: 2g

DESSERTS
RECIPES

PREP TIME

10 minutes

COOKING TIME

0 Minutes

SERVINGS

2

1) Greek Yogurt Parfait
with Berries

A refreshing and simple dessert, perfect for a quick, healthy treat.

INGREDIENTS

- 1 cup Greek yogurt (plain, non-fat)
- 1/2 cup mixed berries (strawberries, blueberries, raspberries)
- 2 tablespoons granola (sugar-free)
- 1 teaspoon honey (optional)

PROCEDURE

1. In a glass or bowl, layer half of the Greek yogurt.
2. Add a layer of mixed berries.
3. Add the remaining Greek yogurt.
4. Top with granola and a drizzle of honey if using.
5. Serve immediately and enjoy!

NUTRITIONAL INFORMATION (PER SERVING)

Calories: 150, Protein: 10g, Carbohydrates: 20g, Fat: 2g

2) Chia Seed Pudding
with Almond Milk and Vanilla

A creamy and nutritious dessert that's easy to prepare ahead of time.

INGREDIENTS

- 1 cup unsweetened almond milk
- 3 tablespoons chia seeds
- 1 teaspoon vanilla extract
- 1 tablespoon sugar-free sweetener (optional)

PROCEDURE

1. In a bowl, combine almond milk, chia seeds, and vanilla extract.
2. Stir well to combine.
3. Cover and refrigerate for at least 4 hours or overnight.
4. Stir before serving. Add sweetener if desired.
5. Serve chilled.

NUTRITIONAL INFORMATION (PER SERVING)

Calories: 120, Protein: 4g, Carbohydrates: 10g, Fat: 7g

3) Baked Apples
with Cinnamon

A warm, comforting dessert that's naturally sweet and delicious.

INGREDIENTS

- 4 medium apples
- 1 teaspoon ground cinnamon
- 1/4 cup water
- 1 tablespoon lemon juice
- 1 tablespoon sugar-free sweetener (optional)

PROCEDURE

1. Preheat oven to 350°F (175°C).
2. Core the apples and place them in a baking dish.
3. Sprinkle cinnamon over the apples.
4. Mix water and lemon juice and pour into the baking dish.
5. Add sweetener if using.
6. Bake for 25 minutes until apples are tender.
7. Serve warm.

NUTRITIONAL INFORMATION (PER SERVING)

Calories: 80, Protein: 0g, Carbohydrates: 21g, Fat: 0g

4) Mixed Berry Salad with Mint

A fresh and vibrant dessert that's bursting with flavor.

INGREDIENTS

- 2 cups mixed berries (strawberries, blueberries, raspberries, blackberries)
- 1 tablespoon fresh mint leaves, chopped
- 1 teaspoon lemon juice
- 1 teaspoon honey (optional)

PROCEDURE

1. In a large bowl, combine mixed berries.
2. Add chopped mint leaves and lemon juice.
3. Toss gently to combine.
4. Drizzle with honey if desired.
5. Serve immediately.

NUTRITIONAL INFORMATION (PER SERVING)

Calories: 60, Protein: 1g, Carbohydrates: 15g, Fat: 0g

5) Avocado Chocolate Mousse

A rich and creamy dessert with a hint of chocolate, perfect for satisfying sweet cravings.

INGREDIENTS

- 2 ripe avocados
- 1/4 cup unsweetened cocoa powder
- 1/4 cup almond milk
- 1 teaspoon vanilla extract
- 2 tablespoons sugar-free sweetener

PROCEDURE

1. Scoop the avocado flesh into a blender.
2. Add cocoa powder, almond milk, vanilla extract, and sweetener.
3. Blend until smooth and creamy.
4. Spoon into serving bowls and refrigerate for 30 minutes before serving.
5. Enjoy chilled.

NUTRITIONAL INFORMATION (PER SERVING)

Calories: 180, Protein: 2g, Carbohydrates: 15g, Fat: 15g

6) Cottage Cheese

with Pineapple Chunks

A light and refreshing dessert with a balance of protein and sweetness.

INGREDIENTS

- 1 cup cottage cheese (low-fat)
- 1/2 cup pineapple chunks (fresh or canned in juice, drained)
- 1 tablespoon unsweetened coconut flakes (optional)

PROCEDURE

1. In a bowl, combine cottage cheese and pineapple chunks.
2. Sprinkle with coconut flakes if using.
3. Serve immediately.

NUTRITIONAL INFORMATION (PER SERVING)

Calories: 120, Protein: 14g, Carbohydrates: 15g, Fat: 2g

PREP TIME

10 minutes

COOKING TIME

Chill for 2 hours

SERVINGS

4

7) Sugar-Free Gelatin
with Fresh Fruit

A colorful and fun dessert that's both low in calories and delicious.

INGREDIENTS

- 1 package sugar-free gelatin (any flavor)
- 2 cups boiling water
- 1 cup mixed fresh fruit (strawberries, blueberries, kiwi)

PROCEDURE

1. In a bowl, dissolve gelatin in boiling water.
2. Let it cool to room temperature.
3. Add mixed fruit to the gelatin mixture.
4. Pour into a mold or serving dishes.
5. Refrigerate for at least 2 hours until set.
6. Serve chilled.

NUTRITIONAL INFORMATION (PER SERVING)

Calories: 20, Protein: 2g, Carbohydrates: 4g, Fat: 0g

8) Coconut Macaroons (Sugar-Free)

with Fresh Fruit

A sweet and chewy treat that's perfect for a quick dessert.

INGREDIENTS

- 2 cups unsweetened shredded coconut
- 1/2 cup almond flour
- 1/3 cup sugar-free sweetener
- 3 egg whites
- 1 teaspoon vanilla extract

PROCEDURE

1. Preheat oven to 350°F (175°C).
2. In a bowl, mix coconut, almond flour, and sweetener.
3. In another bowl, beat egg whites until stiff peaks form.
4. Fold egg whites and vanilla extract into the coconut mixture.
5. Drop spoonfuls of the mixture onto a baking sheet lined with parchment paper.
6. Bake for 15 minutes or until golden brown.
7. Cool before serving.

NUTRITIONAL INFORMATION (PER SERVING)

Calories: 70, Protein: 2g, Carbohydrates: 5g, Fat: 5g

PREP TIME

10 minutes

COOKING TIME

0 Minutes

SERVINGS

12 Balls

9) Peanut Butter Protein Balls

A perfect no-bake dessert that's high in protein and deliciously satisfying.

INGREDIENTS

- 1 cup rolled oats
- 1/2 cup peanut butter (natural, no sugar added)
- 1/4 cup honey or sugar-free sweetener
- 1/4 cup protein powder (vanilla or chocolate)
- 1/4 cup mini chocolate chips (sugar-free, optional)

PROCEDURE

1. In a bowl, mix all ingredients until well combined.
2. Roll the mixture into 1-inch balls.
3. Place on a baking sheet lined with parchment paper.
4. Refrigerate for at least 30 minutes before serving.
5. Store in an airtight container in the fridge.

NUTRITIONAL INFORMATION (PER SERVING)

Calories: 100, Protein: 5g, Carbohydrates: 10g, Fat: 5g

PREP TIME

15 minutes

COOKING TIME

30 Minutes + cooling Time

SERVINGS

12

10) Low-Sugar Lemon Cheesecake Bites

A tangy and creamy dessert that's low in sugar and high in flavor.

INGREDIENTS

- 1 cup almond flour
- 3 tablespoons butter, melted
- 8 oz cream cheese (low-fat, softened)
- 1/4 cup sugar-free sweetener
- 1 teaspoon lemon zest
- 1 tablespoon lemon juice
- 1 teaspoon vanilla extract
- 1 egg

PROCEDURE

1. Preheat oven to 350°F (175°C).
2. In a bowl, mix almond flour and melted butter.
3. Press the mixture into the bottom of a lined muffin tin to form crusts.
4. In another bowl, beat cream cheese until smooth.
5. Add sweetener, lemon zest, lemon juice, vanilla extract, and egg. Mix well.
6. Spoon the cream cheese mixture over the crusts.
7. Bake for 20 minutes until set.
8. Let cool, then refrigerate for at least 2 hours before serving.
9. Enjoy chilled.

NUTRITIONAL INFORMATION (PER SERVING)

Calories: 120, Protein: 4g, Carbohydrates: 5g, Fat: 10g

11) Almond Flour Brownies

These almond flour brownies are rich, fudgy, and perfect for satisfying your sweet tooth without spiking your blood sugar.

INGREDIENTS

- 1 ½ cups almond flour
- 1/3 cup cocoa powder
- ½ teaspoon baking powder
- ¼ teaspoon salt
- ½ cup unsweetened applesauce
- ½ cup erythritol
- 2 large eggs
- 1 teaspoon vanilla extract

PROCEDURE

1. Preheat your oven to 350°F (175°C). Line an 8x8 inch baking dish with parchment paper.
2. In a large bowl, mix almond flour, cocoa powder, baking powder, and salt.
3. In another bowl, combine applesauce, erythritol, eggs, and vanilla extract.
4. Mix the wet ingredients into the dry ingredients until well combined.
5. Pour the batter into the prepared baking dish and spread evenly.
6. Bake for 25 minutes or until a toothpick inserted into the center comes out clean.
7. Let cool before cutting into squares.

NUTRITIONAL INFORMATION (PER SERVING)

Calories: 110, Carbs: 8g, Protein: 4g, Fat: 7g

12) Raspberry Chia Jam
on Whole Grain Crackers

Enjoy a refreshing snack with homemade raspberry chia jam on crunchy whole grain crackers.

INGREDIENTS

- 1 cup fresh raspberries
- 1 tablespoon chia seeds
- 1 tablespoon water
- 8 whole grain crackers

PROCEDURE

1. In a small saucepan, heat raspberries over medium heat until they break down and become syrupy, about 5 minutes.
2. Stir in chia seeds and water. Let it sit for 5 minutes to thicken.
3. Spread the chia jam on whole grain crackers.

NUTRITIONAL INFORMATION (PER SERVING)

Calories: 60, Carbs: 12g, Protein: 1g, Fat: 2g

13) Frozen Yogurt Bark

with Blueberries

This frozen yogurt bark is a delightful, cooling treat packed with antioxidants.

INGREDIENTS

- 2 cups plain Greek yogurt
- 1 tablespoon honey
- 1 cup fresh blueberries

PROCEDURE

1. Line a baking sheet with parchment paper.
2. Mix Greek yogurt and honey in a bowl until well combined.
3. Spread the yogurt mixture evenly on the baking sheet.
4. Sprinkle blueberries on top.
5. Freeze for at least 2 hours until firm.
6. Break into pieces and enjoy.

NUTRITIONAL INFORMATION (PER SERVING)

Calories: 50, Carbs: 6g, Protein: 4g, Fat: 1g

PREP TIME

10 minutes

COOKING TIME

0 Minutes

SERVINGS

12 Balls

14) Pumpkin Spice Energy Balls

These pumpkin spice energy balls are a perfect bite-sized treat with a burst of autumn flavor.

INGREDIENTS

- 1 cup oats
- ¼ cup pumpkin puree
- ¼ cup almond butter
- 1 tablespoon chia seeds
- 1 tablespoon honey
- 1 teaspoon pumpkin pie spice

PROCEDURE

1. In a bowl, mix all ingredients until well combined.
2. Roll the mixture into 1-inch balls.
3. Refrigerate for at least 30 minutes before serving.

NUTRITIONAL INFORMATION (PER SERVING)

Calories: 70, Carbs: 9g, Protein: 2g, Fat: 3g

15) Dark Chocolate Dipped Strawberries

Indulge in these dark chocolate dipped strawberries for a guilt-free treat.

INGREDIENTS

- 10 large strawberries
- ½ cup dark chocolate chips

PROCEDURE

1. Melt dark chocolate chips in the microwave in 30-second intervals until smooth.
2. Dip each strawberry into the melted chocolate and place on a parchment-lined tray.
3. Let the chocolate set at room temperature or refrigerate for faster results.

NUTRITIONAL INFORMATION (PER SERVING)

Calories: 50, Carbs: 7g, Protein: 1g, Fat: 3g

PREP TIME

5 minutes

COOKING TIME

0 Minutes

SERVINGS

2

16) Apple Slices

with Cinnamon and Greek Yogurt

A simple and quick snack that's nutritious and satisfying.

INGREDIENTS

- 1 apple, sliced
- ½ teaspoon ground cinnamon
- ½ cup plain Greek yogurt

PROCEDURE

1. Arrange apple slices on a plate.
2. Sprinkle with ground cinnamon.
3. Serve with a side of Greek yogurt for dipping.

NUTRITIONAL INFORMATION (PER SERVING)

Calories: 80, Carbs: 15g, Protein: 5g, Fat: 1g

17) Low-Carb Berry Crumble

A delicious dessert with a crunchy topping and juicy berry filling.

INGREDIENTS

- 2 cups mixed berries
- 2 tablespoons almond flour
- 2 tablespoons chopped almonds
- 1 tablespoon coconut oil
- 1 tablespoon erythritol
- ½ teaspoon cinnamon

PROCEDURE

1. Preheat oven to 350°F (175°C).
2. Place mixed berries in a baking dish.
3. In a bowl, combine almond flour, chopped almonds, coconut oil, erythritol, and cinnamon.
4. Sprinkle the topping over the berries.
5. Bake for 25 minutes until golden and bubbly.

NUTRITIONAL INFORMATION (PER SERVING)

Calories: 90, Carbs: 8g, Protein: 2g, Fat: 6g

18) Sugar-Free Vanilla Pudding

Enjoy a creamy and satisfying sugar-free vanilla pudding.

INGREDIENTS

- 2 cups unsweetened almond milk
- ¼ cup cornstarch
- 1 tablespoon erythritol
- 1 teaspoon vanilla extract

PROCEDURE

1. In a saucepan, whisk together almond milk, cornstarch, and erythritol.
2. Cook over medium heat, stirring constantly until the mixture thickens.
3. Remove from heat and stir in vanilla extract.
4. Pour into serving dishes and chill for at least 2 hours.

NUTRITIONAL INFORMATION (PER SERVING)

Calories: 60, Carbs: 10g, Protein: 1g, Fat: 2g

PREP TIME

15 minutes

COOKING TIME

0 minutes (chill for 1 hour)

SERVINGS

12 truffles

19) Chocolate Avocado Truffles

These chocolate avocado truffles are rich, creamy, and packed with healthy fats.

INGREDIENTS

- 1 ripe avocado
- ½ cup dark chocolate chips, melted
- 1 tablespoon cocoa powder
- 1 tablespoon erythritol
- 1 teaspoon vanilla extract

PROCEDURE

1. In a bowl, mash the avocado until smooth.
2. Stir in melted chocolate, cocoa powder, erythritol, and vanilla extract until well combined.
3. Refrigerate the mixture for 1 hour.
4. Roll into 1-inch balls and enjoy.

NUTRITIONAL INFORMATION (PER SERVING)

Calories: 70, Carbs: 4g, Protein: 1g, Fat: 6g

20) Ricotta Cheese
with Cinnamon and Greek Yogurt

A simple, yet elegant dessert that pairs creamy ricotta with the sweetness of honey and the crunch of almonds.

INGREDIENTS

- ½ cup ricotta cheese
- 1 tablespoon honey
- 2 tablespoons sliced almonds

PROCEDURE

1. Divide ricotta cheese into two serving bowls.
2. Drizzle with honey.
3. Sprinkle with sliced almonds.

NUTRITIONAL INFORMATION (PER SERVING)

Calories: 150, Carbs: 10g, Protein: 7g, Fat: 9g

PREP TIME

15 minutes

COOKING TIME

0 minutes

SERVINGS

12 bites

21) Carrot Cake Energy Bites

These Carrot Cake Energy Bites are a delicious and healthy snack option, packed with flavors reminiscent of a classic carrot cake. Perfect for a quick bite without the sugar rush.

INGREDIENTS

- 1 cup grated carrots
- 1 cup rolled oats
- 1/2 cup almond flour
- 1/4 cup raisins
- 1/4 cup chopped walnuts
- 1/4 cup unsweetened shredded coconut
- 1/4 cup almond butter
- 1/4 cup sugar-free maple syrup
- 1 tsp vanilla extract
- 1 tsp ground cinnamon
- 1/4 tsp ground nutmeg

PROCEDURE

1. In a large bowl, combine the grated carrots, oats, almond flour, raisins, walnuts, and shredded coconut.
2. In a separate bowl, mix together the almond butter, sugar-free maple syrup, vanilla extract, cinnamon, and nutmeg until smooth.
3. Pour the wet ingredients into the dry ingredients and mix until well combined.
4. Roll the mixture into 12 small bites and refrigerate for at least 30 minutes before serving.

NUTRITIONAL INFORMATION (PER SERVING)

80 calories, 3g fat, 11g carbs, 2g fiber, 2g protein

PREP TIME

10 minutes

COOKING TIME

25 minutes

SERVINGS

4

22) Baked Pears
with Walnuts and Cinnamon

Baked Pears with Walnuts and Cinnamon is a simple yet elegant dessert that's perfect for satisfying your sweet tooth without the added sugar.

INGREDIENTS

- 2 ripe pears, halved and cored
- 1/4 cup chopped walnuts
- 2 tbsp sugar-free maple syrup
- 1 tsp ground cinnamon

PROCEDURE

1. Preheat your oven to 350°F (175°C).
2. Place the pear halves in a baking dish, cut side up.
3. Sprinkle the walnuts evenly over the pears.
4. Drizzle the sugar-free maple syrup over the pears and walnuts.
5. Sprinkle with cinnamon.
6. Bake for 25 minutes or until the pears are tender.

NUTRITIONAL INFORMATION (PER SERVING)

120 calories, 5g fat, 18g carbs, 4g fiber, 1g protein

23) No-Bake Coconut Balls

These No-Bake Coconut Balls are a quick and easy treat that combines the rich taste of coconut with a hint of vanilla, perfect for a sweet snack.

INGREDIENTS

- 1 1/2 cups unsweetened shredded coconut
- 1/2 cup coconut flour
- 1/4 cup coconut oil, melted
- 1/4 cup sugar-free maple syrup
- 1 tsp vanilla extract

PROCEDURE

1. In a bowl, mix together the shredded coconut, coconut flour, melted coconut oil, sugar-free maple syrup, and vanilla extract until well combined.
2. Form the mixture into 15 small balls.
3. Refrigerate for at least 30 minutes before serving.

NUTRITIONAL INFORMATION (PER SERVING)

70 calories, 6g fat, 5g carbs, 3g fiber, 1g protein

24) Low-Sugar Chocolate Chia Pudding

This Low-Sugar Chocolate Chia Pudding is a creamy, chocolatey dessert that's both healthy and satisfying, perfect for a diabetic-friendly treat.

INGREDIENTS

- 1/4 cup chia seeds
- 1 1/2 cups unsweetened almond milk
- 2 tbsp unsweetened cocoa powder
- 2 tbsp sugar-free maple syrup
- 1 tsp vanilla extract

PROCEDURE

1. In a bowl, whisk together the almond milk, cocoa powder, sugar-free maple syrup, and vanilla extract until well combined.
2. Stir in the chia seeds.
3. Cover and refrigerate for at least 4 hours or overnight, until the pudding has thickened.
4. Stir before serving.

NUTRITIONAL INFORMATION (PER SERVING)

100 calories, 6g fat, 12g carbs, 10g fiber, 4g protein

PREP TIME

10 minutes

COOKING TIME

0

SERVINGS

2

25) Strawberry Banana Smoothie Bowl

This Strawberry Banana Smoothie Bowl is a refreshing and nutritious way to start your day or enjoy as a mid-day snack, full of natural sweetness and vitamins.

INGREDIENTS

- 1 cup frozen strawberries
- 1 frozen banana
- 1/2 cup unsweetened almond milk
- 1/2 cup plain Greek yogurt
- 1 tbsp chia seeds

PROCEDURE

1. In a blender, combine the frozen strawberries, frozen banana, almond milk, and Greek yogurt.
2. Blend until smooth and creamy.
3. Pour into bowls and sprinkle with chia seeds.

NUTRITIONAL INFORMATION (PER SERVING)

150 calories, 3g fat, 28g carbs, 5g fiber, 7g protein

PREP TIME

10 minutes

COOKING TIME

12 Minutes

SERVINGS

12

26) Almond Butter Cookies (Sugar-Free)

These Almond Butter Cookies are a delicious and healthy alternative to traditional cookies, made without any added sugar and perfect for a guilt-free snack.

INGREDIENTS

- 1 cup almond butter
- 1/4 cup sugar-free maple syrup
- 1 egg
- 1 tsp vanilla extract
- 1/2 tsp baking soda

PROCEDURE

1. Preheat your oven to 350°F (175°C).
2. In a bowl, mix together the almond butter, sugar-free maple syrup, egg, vanilla extract, and baking soda until smooth.
3. Drop spoonfuls of the dough onto a baking sheet lined with parchment paper.
4. Flatten each cookie slightly with a fork.
5. Bake for 10-12 minutes or until the edges are golden brown.

NUTRITIONAL INFORMATION (PER SERVING)

90 calories, 8g fat, 3g carbs, 1g fiber, 3g protein

27) Frozen Grapes

Frozen Grapes are a simple, refreshing, and naturally sweet treat that's perfect for cooling down on a hot day.

INGREDIENTS

- 2 cups seedless grapes

PROCEDURE

1. Wash the grapes and pat them dry.
2. Spread the grapes in a single layer on a baking sheet.
3. Freeze for at least 2 hours.
4. Transfer the frozen grapes to a freezer-safe bag for storage.

NUTRITIONAL INFORMATION (PER SERVING)

50 calories, 0g fat, 13g carbs, 1g fiber, 1g protein

PREP TIME

10 minutes

COOKING TIME

0 Minutes

SERVINGS

4

28)Berry Sorbet (Sugar-Free)

This Berry Sorbet is a light and refreshing dessert, made with mixed berries and no added sugar, perfect for a diabetic-friendly treat.

INGREDIENTS

- 2 cups mixed frozen berries
- 1/2 cup water
- 1/4 cup sugar-free maple syrup
- 1 tsp lemon juice

PROCEDURE

1. In a blender, combine the frozen berries, water, sugar-free maple syrup, and lemon juice.
2. Blend until smooth.
3. Pour the mixture into a shallow container and freeze for at least 2 hours.
4. Scoop and serve.

NUTRITIONAL INFORMATION (PER SERVING)

60 calories, 0g fat, 16g carbs, 4g fiber, 1g protein

29)Low-Carb Cheesecake Cups

These Low-Carb Cheesecake Cups are a creamy and delicious dessert that satisfies your cheesecake cravings without the extra carbs and sugar.

INGREDIENTS

- 8 oz cream cheese, softened
- 1/4 cup sugar-free maple syrup
- 1 egg
- 1 tsp vanilla extract
- 1/4 cup almond flour

PROCEDURE

1. Preheat your oven to 350°F (175°C).
2. In a bowl, beat the cream cheese until smooth.
3. Add the sugar-free maple syrup, egg, and vanilla extract, and mix until well combined.
4. Divide the mixture evenly among 6 muffin cups lined with paper liners.
5. Sprinkle almond flour evenly over the tops.
6. Bake for 20 minutes or until set.
7. Cool before serving.

NUTRITIONAL INFORMATION (PER SERVING)

Low-Carb Cheesecake Cups

PREP TIME

15 minutes

COOKING TIME

30 Minutes

SERVINGS

6

30) Sugar-Free Apple Crisp

This Sugar-Free Apple Crisp is a warm and comforting dessert made with sweet apples and a crunchy oat topping, perfect for a healthy after-dinner treat.

INGREDIENTS

- 4 cups peeled and sliced apples
- 1/2 cup rolled oats
- 1/4 cup almond flour
- 1/4 cup chopped walnuts
- 2 tbsp coconut oil, melted
- 2 tbsp sugar-free maple syrup
- 1 tsp ground cinnamon

PROCEDURE

1. Preheat your oven to 350°F (175°C).
2. Place the sliced apples in a baking dish.
3. In a bowl, mix together the oats, almond flour, walnuts, melted coconut oil, sugar-free maple syrup, and cinnamon.
4. Sprinkle the oat mixture evenly over the apples.
5. Bake for 30 minutes or until the apples are tender and the topping is golden brown.

NUTRITIONAL INFORMATION (PER SERVING)

160 calories, 8g fat, 22g carbs, 4g fiber, 2g protein

Manufactured by Amazon.ca
Acheson, AB

15545285R00081